P9-CJX-981

A HIGH TIDE WASHES POINT LOBOS NEAR CARMEL, CALIFORNIA.

Exploring America's
Scenic Highways

CALIFORNIA BREAKERS ROLL ASHORE BELOW HIGHWAY 1.

Prepared by the Special Publications Division
National Geographic Society, Washington, D.C.

Contents

ASPENS FRINGE BOULDER-GROVER ROAD IN UTAH'S DIXIE NATIONAL FOREST.

EXPLORING AMERICA'S SCENIC HIGHWAYS

Contributing Authors: LESLIE ALLEN, TONI EUGENE,
    CHRISTINE ECKSTROM LEE, TOM MELHAM,
    CYNTHIA RUSS RAMSAY, GENE S. STUART,
    JENNIFER C. URQUHART, SUZANNE VENINO
Contributing Photographers: TERRY EILER,
    DEWITT JONES, STEVE WALL

Published by THE NATIONAL GEOGRAPHIC SOCIETY
    GILBERT M. GROSVENOR, *President*
    MELVIN M. PAYNE, *Chairman of the Board*
    OWEN R. ANDERSON, *Executive Vice President*
    ROBERT L. BREEDEN, *Vice President,*
        Publications and Educational Media

Prepared by THE SPECIAL PUBLICATIONS DIVISION
    DONALD J. CRUMP, *Editor*
    PHILIP B. SILCOTT, *Associate Editor*
    WILLIAM L. ALLEN, *Senior Editor*
    MARY ANN HARRELL, *Consulting Editor*

Staff for this Book
    RICHARD M. CRUM, *Managing Editor*
    THOMAS B. POWELL III, *Picture Editor*
    CINDA ROSE, *Art Director*
    JODY BOLT, *Consulting Art Director*
    AMY GOODWIN ALDRICH, MARILYN WILBUR CLEMENT,
        RUTH L. CONNOR, PATRICIA F. FRAKES, GAIL N.
        HAWKINS, ALICE JABLONSKY, BROOKE J. KANE,
        LOUISA B. MAGZANIAN, LUCINDA MOORE, *Researchers*
    AMY GOODWIN ALDRICH, JAN LESLIE COOK,
        PAMELA BLACK TOWNSEND,
        PENELOPE DIAMANTI DE WIDT, *Picture Legend Writers*
    JOHN D. GARST, JR., PATRICIA K. CANTLAY, NEAL C.
        DICKEY, JOSEPH F. OCHLAK, KEVIN Q. STUEBE,
        Map Research, Design, and Production
    ELIZABETH ANN BRAZEROL, *Editorial Assistant*
    CAROL ROCHELEAU CURTIS, *Illustrations Assistant*
    PAM CASTALDI, LYNETTE R. RUSCHAK,
        Designers

Engraving, Printing, and Product Manufacture
    ROBERT W. MESSER, *Manager*
    GEORGE V. WHITE, *Production Manager*
    GEORGE J. ZELLER, JR., *Production Project Manager*
    MARK R. DUNLEVY, DAVID V. SHOWERS,
        GREGORY STORER, *Assistant Production Managers*
    MARY A. BENNETT, *Production Assistant*
    JULIA F. WARNER, *Production Staff Assistant*
    DIANNE T. CRAVEN, SUSAN CROSMAN, LORI E. DAVIE,
        MARY ELIZABETH DAVIS, ANN DI FIORE, JANET A.
        DUSTIN, ROSAMUND GARNER, BERNADETTE L.
        GRIGONIS, VIRGINIA W. HANNASCH, NANCY J.
        HARVEY, JOAN HURST, ARTEMIS S. LAMPATHAKIS,
        KATHERINE R. LEITCH, CLEO E. PETROFF, NANCY E.
        SIMSON, VIRGINIA A. WILLIAMS, *Staff Assistants*
    JAMES B. ENZINNA, JOHN W. HARCHICK, *Indexers*

Library of Congress CIP Data: page 196.

Foreword

All North American highways were scenic highways when settlers first carved them out of the wilderness. But scenery was the last thing the early trailblazers and road builders had in mind. They merely wanted to get from here to there—through forests, over mountains, across rivers, deserts, and plains—the easiest way possible.

We know how the advance of civilization altered or in places demolished the pristine look of the continent—with highways carrying their share of the responsibility. Yet how easy it is even today to drive a few miles from any city (or half a mile from any interstate route) and find byways of beauty and vistas of natural charm. The highways treated in this volume are just a few examples of the nation's roadside riches.

In my youth, a song called "Highways Are Happy Ways" became a popular hit. It is my belief that this book awakens the old feeling of freedom and relaxed enjoyment that highway travel brings to mind.

Last fall, my wife and I toured the Blue Ridge Parkway. This was nostalgia rampant. When we reached Adney Gap, south of Roanoke, we were retracing the first section of the parkway to be opened in Virginia—a section that we first traversed on our honeymoon in 1938.

As an American and a highway buff, I remain after all these years not only captivated by the unsullied intimacy of the Blue Ridge Parkway, but amazed at the magnitude of its concept. Add to its 469 miles the connecting Skyline Drive at its northern end and the Newfound Gap Road at its southern end and you have 608 miles of carefree, commerce-free, fast-lane-free driving pleasure—all beginning a bare 75 miles from the nation's capital. If you were to superimpose on the map of Europe a comparable Alpine Parkway, it would begin 75 miles east of Paris, for instance, and cross northern France, southern Germany, Switzerland, and Austria—ending somewhere in Yugoslavia.

One of the main things you notice about the Blue Ridge Parkway is how often you seem to have it to yourself. Yet more than 15 million people used it for recreation in 1984. It and the Natchez Trace Parkway rank just behind California's Golden Gate Recreational Area as the three most visited places of the National Park Service.

Other journeys in this book take you along state and federal roads for regional tours of nature's glories. One of the routes—U.S. 89—billed itself as "the world's most beautiful highway" in the early '60s when, on assignment for NATIONAL GEOGRAPHIC, I traveled its entire length in one of the nation's first assembly-line motor homes. Look for especially impressive sections of that highway running through two chapters herein.

You probably could tell me of many roads with memorable views that you have discovered. As a nation, we do get around—our collective traveling each year averages more than 12,000 miles per person. In 1983, for example, Americans used their highways to take more than 200 million vacation trips.

America, start your engines, and follow the experienced tour guides in this book as they explore some of their favorite scenic highways.

Ralph Gray

Hairpin curves of Burr Trail challenge a driver as the road switchbacks across Capitol Reef National Park toward Utah's Strike Valley.

DEWITT JONES

Vermont 100:
Autumn's Glory Road

By Leslie Allen   Photographs by Steve Wall

Across autumn's palette, Route 100 bisects Waitsfield, Vermont. The Mad River bends toward the road in this valley of the Green Mountains, where townspeople work to balance rural independence and commercial tourism.

CANADA QUEBEC
U.S. VERMONT
Newport•

Jay Peak +
(100)

Lowell •

Johnson
(15)   SMUGGLERS NOTCH
       STATE PARK
Mt. Mansfield   Morristown
4,393 ft   • Bingham Falls
+   MT. MANSFIELD
    STATE FOREST
       • Stowe
Ricker +   LITTLE RIVER
Mt.   ■ STATE PARK
       • Waterbury

G
R   Mad
E   River
E   Glen
N   □   • Waitsfield

    Sugarbush Valley
M   □ • Warren
O
U   N
N
T
A
I   Rochester •
N   GREEN
S   MOUNTAIN
    NATIONAL
    FOREST
       (100)
       (100A)
       • Plymouth

    GREEN
    MOUNTAIN
    NATIONAL
    FOREST   • Weston

LYE BROOK
WILDERNESS   Stratton
AREA   Mountain
       +

Somerset Reservoir
Mt. Snow +
West Dover •
Wilmington •
(100)

VERMONT
MASSACHUSETTS

0   KILOMETERS   30
0   STATUTE MILES   20

The Green Mountains were named for the colors of summer. Yet the ripeness that balmy days bring to Vermont's forested slopes is only one scene in a drama of contrasts. By August the first cluster of scarlet leaves appears as a harbinger of autumn. Soon the colors advance in ranks toward the starkness of late fall; then dormant months of wintry white yield to the pulsing newness of spring. Nowhere is seasonal change played out more vividly than on the slopes of the Green Mountains. At any time of year they are a great amphitheater of nature, and anywhere along Vermont Route 100, travelers are the audience.

For some 200 miles the highway threads the natural central corridor that lies between the Green Mountains on the west and the lesser hills and ranges on the east. This north-south corduroy of rolling highlands and sinuous river valleys is a landscape so convoluted that local residents tell "flatlanders"—anyone born out of the state—that if Vermont were ironed out, it would equal Texas in size.

The mountains fall short of being awesome, though. Few of their glacially smoothed peaks top 4,000 feet. The slopes, however, long presented a formidable obstacle to east-west migration. The villages that nestle in the region's valleys were among the last settlements in Vermont; dirt roads connecting the towns eventually became Route 100. Until the 1950s, when Vermont's booming ski industry began turning the traditional challenge of geography to profit, the highway defined a region of extreme remoteness. It remained largely unpaved past the middle of this century. Today it is exclusively a state highway, which forms the only major continuous route through the Green Mountains.

One person who remembers the rugged days is Ara Pope. I met him at the beginning of my travels, in the north, where Route 100 starts its southward meanderings just a few miles shy of Canada. Ara was born in 1890, and he moved to the village of Lowell when he was six years old.

"I started driving a team of horses for the Lowell creamery when I was 10," he said. "They made a lot of butter, and I'd drive it up to the shipping point twice a week. That took about eight hours each way, all by myself. I'd spend the night, and come back in the morning with a load of feed." For the princely sum of five cents an hour ("and that was good money") Ara joined a local road crew at age 14. He drove horse-drawn graders in summer and giant snow rollers in winter. "Now there was a cold job. We had to pack down the snow on the roads so kids could get to school."

He recalled landmark events: the widening, graveling, and finally the paving of Route 100 near Lowell; the Model T Fords, among the first cars to use the road; the covered log bridges that gave way to sturdier spans. "So much has changed," he said. "My gosh, the whisky they used to smuggle down the road from Canada during Prohibition. And there were mills and factories everywhere. There was a sawmill, butter tub factory, wagon factory, dressing mill, bobbin mill. They're all gone."

Nonetheless, Route 100's northern reaches retained, for me, the feel of a rural Main Street. Flower boxes, rocking chairs, and drying laundry lined up neatly across the front porches of farmhouses. All manner of

Passage to year-round recreation, Route 100 winds 210 miles through valleys and foothills of the Green Mountains, which divide Vermont into eastern and western sections. The highway leads to ski resorts, hiking paths, fishing streams, and forests and parks that fill October days with blazing color.

roadside sales were constantly in progress. Homemade signs advertised yard sales, barn sales, garage sales, porch sales, and just plain sales. One man showed me a few of the dozens of old bicycles he'd acquired and spiffed up for resale; another specialized in recycled hubcaps. An elderly woman displayed lovely handmade quilts.

Beyond the road, undulating patterns of new-mown hay crept up the slopes of the Green Mountains, which rise sporadically here in the north before acquiring a steady elevation to the south. The corn harvest was under way. It was September, a time of intense activity in a dairying region where the growing season is as short as winter is long and harsh.

"What you do all summer is get ready for winter," said dairy farmer Gertrude Lepine, her eyes searching for a sun that refused to shine on her haying efforts. "You store feed, get your wood supply in, fill your barns, harvest your crops, in addition to milking the cows twice a day."

Frost had already taken a nip at the handsome hillside farmstead of the Lepine family in Morristown, and Gertrude was relying on her two sisters for help with the field chores before winter set in. In the meantime, her 85-year-old mother, Imelda, was busily canning and freezing fruits and vegetables from the garden.

The family's self-sufficiency was born of necessity and nurtured by isolation. "You can just imagine what it used to be like," Gertrude laughed. "We didn't get electricity until 1943. When the power used to go out, I had to hand milk 60 cows and worry about cooling the milk. And money," she continued, "we didn't worry about it because we didn't have any! Mother made our clothes from grain bags, discarded clothing, or wool from our sheep."

Pointing downslope, Gertrude explained that she was trying to open up new parcels of the farm's 800 acres to meadow. She had already spent six summers, between chores, on one six-acre plot felling trees, hefting stones, and seeing to the bulldozing of boulders and tree stumps that are the historical headache of New England's farmers. "There's a great sense of achievement in clearing the land," she said. "It makes you appreciate what your forefathers did around here."

Little more than a century ago, three-fourths of Vermont was open land. Owners had cleared it for farming and dairying, and later used it to graze Merino sheep. The burning of timber yielded cash crops, potash and charcoal, and logging became important to Vermont's economy. But in the mid-1800s, the scene changed dramatically as fertile virgin fields in the Midwest and new urban industries elsewhere lured thousands of Vermonters away from their thin-soiled, hilly tracts. So far has the pendulum swung in one century that the ratio of farm to forest has been completely reversed: Three-quarters of Vermont is now wooded. Agriculture, however, remains an important part of the state's economy.

During my travels I learned to read the Route 100 landscape for its subtle historical subplots. My first lesson took place near Waterbury, in Little River State Park where I spent a day hiking along the logging trails and town roads of Ricker Mountain, an abandoned community.

Low stone walls rambled across the slopes; crumbling foundations and cellar holes, still shaded by homey lilac bushes and butternut trees, marked the homesites of Ricker Mountain's 19th-century sawyers and subsistence farmers. A cigar-shaped boiler, some band saws, and a few wheels and pulleys were what remained of the Waterbury Last Block Company, a sawmill. It seemed incredible that a fair-size community had eked out a living on such unforgiving terrain. But it stretched the imagination even more to think that most of this wooded land was still cleared half a century ago, when Ricker Mountain's last residents left.

"It takes work to maintain a field here," writes Charles Johnson in *The Nature of Vermont*. "A clearing will not long remain if untended, for the natural momentum is toward building the forest, following the various paths of succession: field to shrubs to forest is a continuous evolution. . . ." I saw the various phases of growth in progress on Ricker Mountain when I came upon an abrupt change in the forest, an acre devoid of trees. Hardwoods had covered this tract until a few decades ago, when beavers dammed a nearby stream and created a pond that engulfed the trees and killed them. Eventually silt and dead leaves and other organic matter filled the pond, and it dried up. In the clearing, blackberry shrubs, goldenrod, and saplings were now taking over, and in another 50 years or so, hardwoods would again stand here.

Elsewhere, I came across quaking aspens and spindly paper birches, two of the "pioneers" that replace shrubs as the progression continues. The presence of these trees, which thrive in burned-over land, indicated that this area had probably been scorched some time ago by a wildfire. Scarce stands of white pine, Vermont's most notable pioneer, clustered in the rocky soil of the mountain. And stretching away to all points were the stately beeches, ashes, sugar maples, and other hardwoods of the mature forest that the area's first settlers also saw.

Much of Route 100 borders the 295,007 acres of the Green Mountain National Forest and several state forests. These woodlands provide 200 million board feet of lumber to Vermont's economy each year. In addition to traditional demands served by lumbering, such as housing and furniture, is the demand created by wood-burning stoves. Vermont's power companies are also experimenting with the use of wood chips to generate electric power; in Mount Mansfield State Forest, near Stowe, I saw a chipping machine at work. It looked like a fearsome mechanized version of "Sesame Street's" Cookie Monster as it devoured large branches in a single gulp and spat them out as tiny fragments seconds later. Meanwhile, many farmers still tap their sugar maples each spring in the arduous rite that gives Vermont one of the nation's largest crops of maple syrup.

But the real gold is in the leaves themselves, when fall brings a sprightly display of color to foliage and legions of "leaf peepers" to appreciate it. Inns and motels fill up; travel officials issue daily "foliage reports," and in country stores—the social centers in all the little towns—people pass the time predicting when "peak foliage" will occur. In southern Vermont, it happens almost always around Columbus Day weekend.

In this land of legendary autumn, Route 100 provides unexcelled viewing. For a week it was as though my contact lenses had turned to tiny prisms. In the valleys, with mountains thrusting up all around, each glance brought an eyeful of color. Then as the road labored upward, the colors closed in until, at a summit, they splashed away in vibrant waves.

"These are the right kind of trees, hardwoods, for good color. Winter comes on quickly here, so the leaves also change color quickly." Speaking was Charles Johnson, Vermont's state naturalist. I had been wondering what, scientifically, the fall foliage was all about, and during a ride along Route 100 one October day, Charles was explaining. "But the underlying reason for the change," he said, "has to do with day length. As days become shorter after the summer solstice—around June 21—each tree begins to make preparations to shut down operations in the fall." The result is that eventually many of the minerals and sugars in the leaves make their way to the trunk and roots for winter storage. The leaves dry out as layers of new tissue start to seal them off from their branches. At the same time, different pigments become responsible for different colors.

"When you see a green leaf turning yellow, what's happening is that the chlorophyll that made it green is dying and starting to expose different pigments, called carotenoids," Charles said. One of these, carotene, also colors carrots; another one, xanthophyll, which also brightens egg yolks and canary feathers, yields a different yellow color in leaves. "But the reds are another story," he continued. "Those pigments are called anthocyanins. They are the same kind that you see in apples and tomatoes." The production of these bits of coloring matter in leaves is inhibited by sugar. In autumn the manufacturing of sugar shuts down in the leaves. When the sugar disappears, the reds appear.

Warm, sunny days and frosty nights enhance the production of anthocyanins and concentrate the colors in the leaves. The fluctuating temperature sets hillsides ablaze in reds and oranges. By the second half of October, though, the gala is ending and the long winter approaches. Then, Route 100 is reincarnated as Vermont's "Ski Highway." The slopes just west of the road belong to some of the East's major ski resorts; they begin with Jay Peak near the Canadian border and run from Stowe all the way to Mount Snow near the Massachusetts line.

As an American industry, downhill skiing began at Stowe after a handful of men began promoting the sport half a century ago. One of them was Perry H. Merrill, who retired in 1966 after 37 years as Vermont's commissioner of forests and parks. "Back in the early 1920s, most everyone was getting around on snowshoes," he told me. Only a few people skied at all, and that was chiefly cross-country. There were no downhill trails. In 1921 a winter carnival brought a toboggan slide, ski jump, and skating rink to Stowe. At the same time, Perry was studying under a fellowship at the Royal College of Forestry in Stockholm, Sweden.

"I got the concept for skiing as a big sport over there," he said. "My whole vision was based on what was already going on in Europe. So I thought, wouldn't it be nice if I could start something when I came back. The Depression finally gave me the chance. I had workers from 20 Civilian Conservation Corps camps under my direction, and that gave me manpower; so I put the men at Waterbury Camp to work building the first downhill trail on Mount Mansfield in Stowe." The trail was free to the public. Few skiers used it, but it drew private investors to the area.

I asked Perry where the ski industry would be without the Depression and the Civilian Conservation Corps (CCC), a program that President Franklin D. Roosevelt had started to create jobs for the unemployed.

"It would've been delayed a good many years, probably," Perry replied. "People thought I was crazy at the time. They kept telling me this would never amount to anything."

FOLLOWING PAGES: *West Branch Brook sculpts a shady ravine close to Smugglers Notch State Park on Route 108. Such idyllic hideaways spark tourism, second only to manufacturing as Vermont's chief livelihood.*

One of Mount Mansfield's popular ski runs is named for Perry. Another honors Charlie Lord, who as a young engineer and foreman under Perry in the CCC surveyed the mountain and planned its first trails.

"Getting back up the mountain for another run was a different matter in the early days," Charlie said. "You had to climb, and it was a good skier who could make two runs a day." A rope tow was installed, and then a chair lift—almost unheard of in the East—to carry skiers to the mountaintop. "It was rather a bold venture," Charlie said. Inaugurated in 1940, the chair lift was custom-built by a company that manufactured tramways for mines.

Today skiers on Mount Mansfield, Vermont's highest peak, are faced with a choice of 35 runs and 10 lifts and tows, including a gondola. It's much the same at the other major resorts, where machine-made snow extends skiing from fall through spring. The effect of all this on some of the nearby towns has been enormous. Warren, for instance, was a quaint but depressed town in the Mad River Valley until Sugarbush opened in 1958. Three years earlier, Warren's stretch of Route 100 was unpaved. Customers at the general store sometimes settled accounts by handing over deeds to fallow lands. Today the road is paved, a fraction of an acre goes for thousands of dollars, and the store stocks an array of fine foods and wines as Warren retains its old charm in a newly sophisticated guise.

Change is even more pronounced in neighboring Waitsfield. In the 1830s, output from riverside mills joined farm production to boost the

Rocky steps of Bingham Falls spill the West Branch Brook. Each autumn, the flashy leaves of sugar maples (above), yellow birch, and many other hardwoods along Route 100 attract thousands of admiring motorists.

town's prosperity. Twenty years later, lacking a major rail connection, Waitsfield began a slow decline, only to reemerge in the 1950s and '60s as the service center for skiers at Mad River Glen and Sugarbush.

One of the few Route 100 towns to escape the threat of runaway commercialization is Plymouth, the birthplace of President Calvin Coolidge. The preservation of his homestead, which lies within the town's historic district of Plymouth Notch, is managed by state agencies. In many other towns, however, local organizations work at safeguarding the welcoming atmosphere of rural life.

"My whole idea when I started this in 1957 was to do everything as simply, quietly, and traditionally as possible," Ann Day Heinzerling told me. She owns and manages Knoll Farm Country Inn, a turn-of-the-century farmhouse that stands on 150 rolling acres near Waitsfield. The inn contains only four guest rooms, which are sometimes booked a year in advance. "We could fill up ten times over if we got bigger and hired more help," Ann said. "But we intentionally keep it small." Upstairs, wildflowers from highland meadows added cheer to rooms filled with antiques. Downstairs, a fragrant loaf of dill and onion bread was rising on the kitchen's stove. Most of the vegetables, meat, and eggs served at Knoll Farm are grown there. On the dining room walls hang paintings of the old barn, the work of various guests. For the musically inclined, the inn maintains a 19th-century pump organ in the living room and another organ and a player piano in the sitting room; for bookworms there is a well-stocked library.

Outdoors, guests may help with farm chores or take a ride in an antique buggy or in a sleigh. Ann leads nature walks, and depending on the season, there are horseback riding, cross-country skiing, snowshoeing, and sledding. "Even though the valley has changed," Ann said, "Knoll Farm hasn't. People who come here say it's like going back to their childhood home, or back to grandmother's. I'm very sentimental, and I feel an obligation to our guests to keep things deeply traditional."

Those who visit and then choose to live in the shadow of the Green Mountains come for many reasons. For some, settling here is the expression of a long-held private dream. "I just finally gave myself what I wanted," said Jon Zachadnyk. He operates Zack's On the Rocks, a castlelike inn and restaurant in Montgomery Center. Dressed in a purple caftan, Zack shows dinner guests into rooms zanily decorated to theatrical effect. "I'm a frustrated actor who created his own theater," he explained. In another town, I met Carl Lobel, a young lawyer who had left New Jersey to sell antiques and collect old mechanical toys; his house held dozens of wind-up comic characters, including Mickey Mouses, L'il Abners, and Popeyes. Some residents adopt more traditional, regional themes. Earl Cooley, a retired asbestos miner in Johnson, was successfully growing Tolman Sweet, Red Astrachan, and Fameuse, tasty varieties of apples no longer available commercially.

"Everybody said you can't grow fruit here," Earl told me, "but people did long ago, so why shouldn't I?"

Many residents of Route 100's corridor are looking to the past for solutions to a modern problem: high-priced energy. Windmills dot slopes, catching the breeze to churn out low-cost electrical power, and water wheels of old restored mills shadow streams, dipping into rushing currents to crank out profitable kilowatts. Nature also powers the artistic imaginations of many residents here. Waterfalls that tumble through the Green Mountains, for instance, inspire jeweler Bill Butler. Like many friends I made during my travels, Bill was eager to take a day off and show me a scenic hideaway off Route 100. "Just don't tell people where it is," he warned, "or it'll never be the same."

We walked into the woods and made our way down a steep path. There, at the end of the trail, waterfalls, chutes, and pools stretched as far as the eye could see. With the whole place to ourselves, we spent the afternoon scrambling over mossy rocks from one fall to the next. The rocks were shaped by the water's pounding and sculpted into countless delicate contours. Here, I saw delicate arches; there, swirling eddies hollowed small caves. Everywhere, in the patterns and shapes of rock, water, and erupting foam I clearly saw the line and flow of Bill's own work.

Arts and crafts flourish in many communities on Route 100. The carefully restored town of Weston, for instance, features two cultural centers that reflect the evolution of towns along the route. One, the Old Mill Museum, displays antique tools of artisans while providing workshops for several of Weston's craftspeople, and the other, Weston's playhouse, was

Bounty of pumpkins and squash—and Jeanna, 2—blesses the family farm of Judy Jensen, who sells produce to Route 100 travelers in Rochester.

FOLLOWING PAGES: *High-ridge riders, outside the town of Johnson, cross a pasture on Vermont's only turf farm. Of all the New England states, Vermont relies the most heavily on agricultural goods as a source of income.*

originally a church. The history of Route 100 itself reflects change brought about by new opportunities. Until the 1960s the highway ended a few miles north of Weston, and the road from there south to the Massachusetts border was called Route 8. But with the growth of Green Mountains tourism, business owners and state officials quickly perceived the economic advantages that a single state highway, edging the mountains almost from border to border, could bring.

Motoring tourists whom the road funnels into Vermont usually end their journey along the state's southern reaches. This area extends southward from Weston and attracts huge numbers of skiers and part-time dwellers, especially around West Dover and Wilmington. The road here travels along and through some of the most remote terrain of the Green Mountain National Forest. In the area, during an overnight hike to the top of Stratton Mountain, the profound contrasts that have shaped the state became all the more vivid to me.

It was the end of my trip and late autumn; few other hikers braved the chilly gusts that roared like rough surf and sent falling leaves into long upward spirals. The path was a stretch of the Long Trail, which, like a hiker's Route 100, follows the Green Mountains the entire length of Vermont. The way was not always densely wooded; I passed a marked site where 15,000 people had gathered in 1840 to hear orator Daniel Webster speak out for the Whigs, the party backing William Henry Harrison for President. Now, the view hardly opened up at all. I reached the summit several hours later and climbed out of the fog to the top of an old fire tower built by the Civilian Conservation Corps.

Everything I saw seemed to tell the story of development and preservation, the opposing forces that are pulling at the fiber of Vermont. Just on the other side of the peak, Stratton's chair lifts waited in silent ranks for the skiers who would soon arrive; in another direction, I saw pristine Stratton Pond, a hiker's haven. Much larger, Somerset Reservoir to the south serves the water needs of an expanding population while, nearby, the federally designated Lye Brook Wilderness Area protects the primeval isolation of 15,600 acres of national forest.

In many places along Route 100, I heard people discussing what combination of farm, forest, and town, mountain and valley makes for the best scenery—and the wisest course for development. Such matters are of long-standing interest. Back in 1936, Vermonters voted in town meetings on a federal proposal to build a national scenic highway through the Green Mountains. The model for the byway was to be the Skyline Drive in Virginia's Blue Ridge Mountains.

With characteristic independence, and some fears of environmental threats to their beloved mountains, the voters said "no" to the federal government. Today geographic fortune and economic opportunity have given Vermonters the closest thing to such a parkway. From untouched wilderness to farm, village, and ski slope, Route 100 weds scenery to history and man to nature, in time as well as in space.

Five cords stored by Earnest Earle include cuts of oak and maple. He and his wife, Evelyn, use wood almost exclusively for winter cooking and heating. They will burn all the logs by spring on their farm in northern Vermont.

*"Best swimming hole on the Mad River," say these four local outdoor experts. On
a September afternoon in the town limits of Warren, Aaron Groom, Max Popowicz,
Matthew Groom, and Chris Tripodi (left to right) sun themselves on the window ledge
of a century-old covered bridge. The restored structure straddles a spur of Route 100.
Matthew (above) hurls himself from the window and drops 20 feet into the river. His
mother checked the depth of the water and considers it safe for the boys to jump from
the bridge, but quickly adds, "I wouldn't let them dive in."*

Bare in March snow, sugar maples drip sap into buckets on Spring Brook Farm in Reading. The ox-drawn sled carries the raw material to the sugar house (below, left), where boiling and straining yield tasty syrup, a major Vermont product.

FOLLOWING PAGES: *Less than ten miles from the Canadian border, a sunset skier begins her downhill run on Jay Peak. Most of Vermont's alpine ski areas lie off Route 100 in the Green Mountains, birthplace of America's ski-lift tradition.*

Blue Ridge Parkway:
Highland Journey

By Suzanne Venino   Photographs by Steve Wall

Riding the backbone of the southern Appalachians, the Blue Ridge Parkway slips past a Christmas-tree farm in Virginia. The ribbon of road binds miles of mountain splendor along forested reaches of the nation's early frontier.

loating freely at the whim of the winds, I'm gazing down at the land from the tiny basket of a hot-air balloon. Forested mountains roll toward the horizon like waves in a surging sea, and rays of silver sunlight burst through clouds in a dramatic parting gesture to the day. From my airborne perch, the asphalt road below looks like a thin ribbon winding through North Carolina's Asheville Valley. An ordinary road? Not by any means. Topping mountain crests, dipping into river valleys, rambling through farmlands and vast tracts of national forests, the Blue Ridge Parkway has been painstakingly crafted by human hands·to reveal the natural beauty of the southern Appalachians.

To enjoy the road up close, I traded my balloon for a car and leisurely followed the parkway's 469 miles through the highlands of Virginia and North Carolina. The dogwood still showed white among the other trees as I pulled away from milepost zero at Rockfish Gap, Virginia, in late spring. Driving south along the crests of the Blue Ridge Mountains, I could glance out to my left and see the foothills of the Piedmont. To the west the Blue Ridge fell away to the sweep of the Shenandoah Valley, a verdant mosaic of farms, towns, and factories framed by the ragged profile of the Allegheny Mountains.

The scenery changed with almost every bend of the road: A sheer rock bluff shadowed the right-of-way; a valley sank out of sight; a tunnel of trees opened onto a field of wildflowers. I would soon discover that this scenic medley had been carefully orchestrated.

"The parkway was planned, designed, and landscaped for visual variety," Robert A. Hope, chief landscape architect since 1969, told me when I visited parkway headquarters in Asheville, North Carolina.

In the 1930s, survey teams of engineers and landscape architects selected the route after studying topographical maps to find the most varied sights and interesting geologic features. When maps were unavailable, they scouted the countryside, asking mountain folk along the way: "Where's the best view?" As construction crews carved the roadway through the mountains, they followed strict specifications that kept damage to the natural setting at a minimum. Landscape architects added the finishing touches by supervising the planting of native trees and bushes to hide the scars of road building.

"Every mile of the parkway is landscaped. Yet it's so natural that few travelers would ever guess it," Mr. Hope said as he showed me reams of blueprints. "These show the size, spacing, and placement of plantings just as the original landscape architect envisioned it. They also indicate where bushes were to be burned away and trees cut down to clear vistas and roadside overlooks.

"The views from overlooks were designed to create a feeling of unlimited horizons, like looking at the world from a balcony. While the road's right-of-way is narrow, averaging only 1,000 feet, we say that the parkway boundary is as far as the eye can see."

The number of people who take in the road's sweeping views has increased from a hundred thousand in 1939 to more than 18 million in 1984.

Landscaped for visual variety, the 469-mile Blue Ridge Parkway ties Shenandoah National Park in Virginia to the Great Smoky Mountains National Park in North Carolina. The federal road gives motorists easy access to quiet woodland retreats far above the clamor of cities.

Administered by the National Park Service, the parkway is actually a long skinny park with 19 recreation areas strung along its length like knots in a rope. Operating from May through October, these areas help carry out the purpose of the road as cited in the "Blue Ridge Parkway News" in 1938. The newsletter, printed to inform mountain people about the new route, described the parkway as "a special kind of road . . . for the pleasure and recreation of those who use it rather than for the business of life."

From sitting under a shade tree to strapping on a hang glider and sailing away on the wind, people on the parkway can find many escapes from the commercial world. At Humpback Rocks, milepost 5.8 in Virginia, many visitors take refuge in history. Here a self-guided trail winds through a re-created homestead of log buildings. In authentic costumes, a Park Service team works as mountain people did a hundred years ago. The staff members make lye soap in a cast-iron pot, cook cornbread in a skillet over an open fire, and fashion farm tools from wood felled in the forest. Visitors wander where they will, and the staff workers answer questions about traditional mountain life as they go about their chores.

Botanists, bird watchers, rock hounds, and rock climbers, as well as history buffs, find the parkway grounds appealing. For hikers the area is paradise. Hundreds of miles of trails braid the region.

I planned a three-day hike along the Appalachian Trail, which for approximately a hundred miles crisscrosses the northern end of the parkway. From Reeds Gap near milepost 14 in Virginia, I followed paint-blazed trees south into George Washington National Forest. A couple came hiking toward me at such a fast pace that I thought they were racing. In a sense they were. By quickening their step, they would be able to gain a day on their 2,138-mile trek from Georgia to Maine. They were Sharon Turk and Bruce Parsons, and they had set out to hike the entire length of the Appalachian Trail in little more than three months. Had they enjoyed their first 800 miles?

"Well, not all the time," admitted Sharon. "Between the bad weather, bugs, and sore feet, sometimes it's not so much fun. But then there are the little surprises, like the bright orange salamanders I saw after a rain the other day."

"Your heart has to be in this," Bruce noted.

"This is my first hiking experience," Sharon said. "It's an adventure, and a challenge too. Seven out of eight people who start out to do the trail don't finish it."

They adjusted their packs and raced off with more than 1,200 miles to go. This was my first time backpacking too, and I had thought 20 miles or so would be plenty. It was. By the second day, after crossing the swinging bridge over the Tye River, I began to creak with stiffness. Slowly I returned to camp with fantasies about a chiropractor who made tent calls.

I had pitched my tent beside a series of waterfalls that danced down moss-green rocks and splashed from pool to pool. Deep and clear, the water looked inviting after a hot day on the trail. I jumped in. Two seconds later I jumped out. It was cold!

The sound of the gurgling water lulled me to sleep. In the morning a wood thrush's rapid *pit-pit-pit* call and a bluebird's *chur chur-lee chur-lee* gently woke me to a world of sunlight and soft hues of green. Elm leaves formed a lacy canopy overhead, and beneath a thick understory of mountain laurel and rhododendron, ferns carpeted the forest floor. Despite my aches and pains, the serene forest soothed my citified soul.

It was hard to believe that this lush woodland had once felt the blade of an ax. Yet these forests were ruthlessly exploited around the turn of the century. Old logging roads and remnants of narrow-gauge railroads speak of the days when men trooped into the hills and took what they wanted of the land. They left behind a denuded terrain. National-forest status now protects immense areas of the southern Appalachians from such uncontrolled harvesting of timber.

For much of its length the Blue Ridge Parkway travels through national forests. It is these expanses of trees that help give the Blue Ridge its name. Oaks, hickory, and other deciduous trees release hydrocarbons through leaf pores during the process of photosynthesis. The escaping moisture hangs over the mountains in a vapor, and ridge lines seem to recede into the distance in hazy shades of blue.

From the heights of George Washington National Forest in Virginia, the parkway descends to its lowest elevation of 646 feet near the James River, milepost 63, and then quickly climbs to nearly 4,000 feet in Jefferson National Forest. At this high elevation, flowers that had long since faded in the lowlands were still blooming in mid-July. Shaggy white blossoms of goat's beard nodded in the breezes, and vibrant orange day lilies leaned toward the sun.

This is bear country, and I kept a sharp eye out for them, especially after I had heard the tale about the hitchhiking bear: "I passed them on the road," recalled Gene Parker, district ranger at the Peaks of Otter recreation area, milepost 86. "A couple in a convertible with a bear in the backseat. The bear was sitting up and riding along just like a person, the wind blowing through its fur.

"They had stopped to see the bear alongside the road," Gene continued, "and the bear hopped right in the car. The couple remained calm and drove to the nearest ranger station, though the woman did keep looking nervously back over her shoulder."

Gene knew the animal. It was Gris, a black bear that Gene had rescued when it was a frightened, motherless cub. Gene raised it with the permission of the game warden. "I tried to keep Gris wild and not let him get too used to humans," Gene said. "But that Gris liked to hang around people; he was getting pretty rambunctious too. He'd show up at picnic areas, and once he invited himself to an evening campfire program." Eventually Gris was escorted to another park.

Besides rescuing bears, parkway rangers fight forest fires, catch criminals, and assist with childbirths. "It's an exciting life," Gene said. "You never know what's going to happen next." Cliff Pendry, now retired after 30 years with the Park Service, recalls chasing bootleggers and moonshiners along the parkway at speeds of 90 to 100 miles per hour.

"Moonshine whiskey was a means of livelihood for many people here in the 1930s. They used the Blue Ridge Parkway to transport it, figurin' they wouldn't get caught 'cause there weren't as many rangers as there were sheriffs in nearby towns," Cliff said. "You could tell them comin' 'cause they drove souped-up Fords with heavy-duty rear springs.

"One moonshiner made two trips a week, worked a schedule regular as a Greyhound bus. I knew where he was loadin' up, and me and the local sheriff was making plans to get him when the 'shiner drove by. I said, 'Fellas, there go our plans, let's get that rascal,' and we lit out after him.

He abandoned the car and took off down the mountain. My partner chased him on foot for the better part of an hour before he finally caught that fella. We later found the car with fruit jars of moonshine stacked like cordwood—about a hundred gallons of whiskey.

"Very little moonshine is made here now," Cliff added. Today rangers have to look out for people sneaking onto parkway land to plant marijuana. And often they have to shoo away couples who view the road as a lovers' lane. "Well, I walked up to one couple who were smoochin'," Cliff said, "and I tapped that ol' boy on the shoulder and said, 'Just what do you figure this parkway was built for?'

" 'Recreation, sir,' the fellow replied."

While the purpose of the parkway is indeed recreation, its construction during the Great Depression served a more practical end. In 1933 it was suggested to President Franklin D. Roosevelt that the Skyline Drive being built through Virginia's Shenandoah National Park be extended southward to link up with the Great Smoky Mountains National Park on the North Carolina-Tennessee border. Construction of such a road would provide jobs for thousands of people in one of the most destitute regions of the country. Congress approved the plan. *(Continued on page 42)*

Steely-eyed bald eagles nest in a refuge near milepost 300 on the parkway in North Carolina. Hunters and natural food poisoned by pesticides have killed off so many of these birds that they rank as endangered in 43 states.

Cherokee Ed Welch prepares to harness his horse for work in hayfields (opposite) on his 500-acre farm east of milepost 469 in North Carolina. The 82-year-old Native American acquired his holdings by purchasing tribal land reclaimed from the federal government by the Cherokee Nation. In 1838, Ed's ancestors hid in the mountains and escaped U. S. troops who drove 15,000 Cherokees from their homeland to Oklahoma Territory in a bitter march known as the Trail of Tears.

Rustic trail leads a hiking family under a Canadian hemlock in the Linville Falls area of North Carolina. A late-blooming trillium (below) touches a leaf of impatiens. Six species of trillium brighten the parkway region from late April to early July. This patch of wildflowers flourishes outside the town of Little Switzerland, so named because its setting resembles the Jura Mountains in Europe.

PRECEDING PAGES: *Cascades ruffle the Linville River south of milepost 316 in North Carolina. In 1827, considering the land unfit for farming, the owner of this granite gorge traded the falls for a suit of homespun clothes.*

Even before the Depression, farm incomes in southern Appalachia averaged only $86 a year. Exploitation by lumber and mining companies and years of farming had eroded the land and depleted the soil. Many households depended on the chestnut harvest to supplement their meager earnings. Each fall entire families would go into the forest to gather sacks of chestnuts to trade for credit at the country store. Before the Depression hit, a fungus blight killed all the chestnut trees.

When a mountain man could find work, wages averaged ten cents an hour. Work as a laborer on the Blue Ridge Parkway paid three times that much. Many breadwinners considered the road job a lifesaver. "I started working on the parkway when I was 24 years old, making nine dollars a week." Talking with me was Cap Ayers, a retired factory worker from Virginia. "They wouldn't let you work but 30 hours a week back then. That way they could put more men to work.

"We didn't have much machinery, had to dig ditches and slope all them banks with hand shovels. One year we killed 17 copperheads."

In his 70s, Cap works for the parkway again, this time as a volunteer playing old-time Appalachian music; it's a home-grown sound that evolved from the traditional tunes of the Scotch-Irish who settled these hills and hollows in the 1700s.

Cap and "the boys"—the youngest of whom is 68—were in fine form the morning I stopped in at the Matthews Cabin, a restored log house at Mabry Mill recreation area, milepost 176. The happy sounds of fiddle, dulcimer, autoharp, and banjo filled the tiny cabin. Someone got to flat-footin', a kind of shuffling dance. Cap broke into a little jig, and I joined in too. The floor boards rocked up and down with us. Others clapped their hands or tapped their feet. Mountain music just makes you feel good!

Behind us the water-powered wheel of the old gristmill kept a steady beat as it ground cornmeal, grits, and buckwheat flour, just as it had done when Ed Mabry ran it. "Lord yes, I knowed Ed Mabry," Cap said. "As boys, we used to go swimmin' in his millpond. He was a good un all right, a hard worker."

Miller, blacksmith, woodworker, and wheelwright, Ed Mabry was typical of the versatile craftsmen found in remote mountain communities. These people were a self-sufficient lot. They had to be. Few roads gave access to the forbidding hills of southern Appalachia, and those that did were rutted dirt trails passable only on foot, horseback, or by wagon. Until the 1930s, when paved roads started inching through the mountains, life here had remained virtually isolated for well over a century. People grew their own food, wove their own cloth, and made their own furniture, tools, and musical instruments. They carved toys for the children, gathered medicinal herbs from the forest, and entertained their families with stories passed down through generations.

After Ed Mabry died in 1936, the Park Service turned his property into one of the many parkway exhibits on mountain culture. The traditional life-style is also treasured along the backcountry roads that branch

---

Billy Joe Lambert bites into a summer treat at his family's produce stand at Boone, North Carolina. In July as many as 400 motorists a day stop here for free country recipes and to buy homegrown vegetables and canned goods.

off the parkway. On highland homesteads women piece quilts in winter and can fresh garden vegetables in summer. People gather for church revivals and weekly square dances; customers in country stores pull up a chair and visit a spell.

Rural ways hold fast along the parkway as it ambles across the Blue Ridge plateau. This rolling terrain begins below Roanoke, Virginia, milepost 121, and extends into North Carolina as far as Grandfather Mountain, milepost 291. White clapboard houses and weathered barns paint a picture of quiet simplicity. Neat fields of corn and cabbage line the road, and Herefords graze in pastures bordered by split-rail fences.

In populated areas such as this, the federal government owns the right-of-way but pays for rights of scenic easement. By this agreement, farmers owning land within sight of the parkway must obtain Park Service approval before making additions or alterations to their property. This keeps the landscape free of billboards, souvenir shops, fast-food stands, or any distraction that would spoil the pastoral scene.

Leaving this rural setting, the parkway rises through open meadows and climbs into the mountains of Pisgah National Forest. Here close to the resort town of Blowing Rock, North Carolina, textile magnate Moses Cone built a magnificent mountaintop retreat in the 1890s. A road-building hobbyist, Mr. Cone laced the estate with miles of bridle paths and carriage trails. His wife's will set aside the 3,600-acre estate as a public "pleasure ground," which was turned over to the Blue Ridge Parkway. Today joggers, horseback riders, and cross-country skiers frequent the 25 miles of trails at the Moses H. Cone Memorial Park, milepost 293. The Cones' stately manor house now serves as a sales shop for artisans of the Southern Highlands Handicraft Guild.

Just a few miles south, I discovered the "missing link." At milepost 300 the road detours, and travelers take North Carolina Route 221 for nine miles around the last section of the parkway still under construction.

"The road was built in scattered bits and pieces, which were eventually linked together," explained Dr. Harley Jolley, historian and noted authority on the Blue Ridge Parkway. "This was done deliberately. Priority was given to sections that would most easily open scenic areas for public use and that would also provide jobs where needed most."

I had met Dr. Jolley at the construction site of the Linn Cove Viaduct. When completed, this sleek cantilevered bridge will S-curve for about a fifth of a mile along the side of Grandfather Mountain. Construction workers swarmed around us.

"In the 1930s it was projected that the parkway would employ 4,000 men for two years," Dr. Jolley said. "As you can see, the parkway is still providing employment."

Political infighting over the route and problems with procuring rights-of-way delayed the start of the parkway for two years, until September 1935. Once work began, engineers found that they had vastly underestimated the difficulties of bushwhacking, bulldozing, and blasting a road through a mountain wilderness. On one 9.4-mile section, crews used 35,000 drill bits to bore holes for the dynamite needed to blast away some 100,000 cubic feet of rock. During World War II, manpower and materials were diverted overseas, and work on the parkway stopped. Disagreement over the right-of-way held up the last section until 1968.

"Years of planning went into the viaduct," Dr. Jolley said. "Engineers and landscape architects puzzled over how to span the mountainside without spoiling the natural setting." He pointed to a big boulder. Lichen, sand myrtle, and a red spruce seedling decorated the rock with the graceful harmony of a Japanese print. "If this were just an ordinary road," he said, "we would have blasted right through that rock. But we wanted to preserve this environment, so we planned the road around it."

Tiptoeing around Grandfather Mountain with more than 10,000 tons of concrete and steel, the Linn Cove Viaduct is as much an engineering feat today as building an entire road through these mountains would have been half a century ago. The final section of parkway is slated for completion in 1987, two years after the road's 50th anniversary. Officials say the Blue Ridge Parkway's total cost will run about 140 million dollars, not far off the 16 million dollars originally authorized, given inflation.

On the road again I turned off at milepost 316. At the Linville Falls recreation area I hiked to the river's edge. On my way I passed stands of hemlock, butternut, and tall virgin pine. The waters of the Linville thunder through narrow rock walls, plunge in a curtain of foam, then placidly flow into Linville Gorge, the deepest canyon in the eastern United States. South of the gorge at milepost 355, State 128 peels off the parkway and leads to the top of Mount Mitchell, named after Elisha Mitchell. In 1857, this noted geologist and botanist died when he fell from a cliff and drowned in a pool while he was attempting to verify measurements of the height of the 6,684-foot peak, the tallest east of the Mississippi.

The parkway rounds Mount Mitchell, leaves the Blue Ridge Mountains, and passes through five other Appalachian ranges: the Black Mountains, the Great Craggies, the Pisgah Ledge, the Great Balsams, and the Plott Balsams. These are ancient hills, some of the oldest on earth. Starting about a billion years ago, repeated folding and faulting heaved the mountains to enormous jagged heights. Ages of erosion have left the southern Appalachians softly rounded and corrugated by deep valleys. When fog fills the hollows, the peaks seem to float like wooded islands in a smoky sea.

As the parkway rolls down the Great Craggies, it leaves Pisgah National Forest and swings southwesterly around the city of Asheville, North Carolina, milepost 382. The road crosses the French Broad River, plays hide and seek through a series of tunnels, and rises again into the forests of Pisgah. At milepost 431 the parkway reaches its highest elevation— 6,053 feet above sea level.

Along these peaks, the rich mantle of deciduous trees gives way to dark evergreen forests of spruce, pine, and balsam. In August, fringes of purple phlox, yellow coneflowers, white elderberry blossoms, and dozens of other flowers seem to turn the parkway into a garden path through the Appalachians. Each year convoys of cars, motorcycles, and recreational vehicles crowd the road as people come to witness the cheerful blossoms of spring or the bright leaves of fall.

For its final ten miles the parkway travels through the Cherokee Indian Reservation. Known officially as the Qualla Boundary, it is home to approximately 5,500 people. Most of them are descendants of Indians who hid in the mountains to escape removal from their native lands when the federal government rounded up eastern tribes for relocation in Oklahoma. Tragically marked by hunger and disease, the forced march westward during the bitter winter of 1838 became known as the Trail of Tears. More than 4,000 Cherokees died along the way.

The handful who remained in North Carolina struggled for existence. Gradually they began buying back their homeland through a white trader who befriended them, and in 1889 the Eastern Band of Cherokees was legally recognized. Today the 57,000-acre Qualla Boundary is a tribally owned preserve held in trust by the federal government.

In the town of Cherokee, I visited the showroom of the Qualla Arts and Crafts Mutual, a cooperative owned and operated by the Indians. "Aside from the Cherokee language, which is still spoken by some and is taught in the schools, the old ways are being kept alive mainly through arts and crafts," said Betty Dupree, the cooperative's executive director. She showed me around the shop, and I admired intricate beadwork, bold basket designs, and wood-carved animals. An unusual piece of pottery caught my eye. It was a kind of double-mouthed pitcher.

"It's a wedding vase," Betty said. Cherokee women still make the vases by hand, carefully molding the clay and smoothing the surface with a moistened stone. By pressing carved wooden paddles into the soft clay, they imprint a design; then they fire the pottery over smoldering wood. The vase I held represented pottery-making skills that have been passed down through a millennium of Cherokee culture.

Here, in the land of Indian craftsmen, the parkway ends on the banks of the Oconaluftee River. The last milepost reads 469, but the road greatly exceeds its measured mileage. Its passage through the mountains opens a corridor onto the ages of culture, history, and grandeur of the southern Appalachians. The Blue Ridge Parkway is no ordinary road. Like a fine piece of Cherokee pottery, it is what it was crafted to be: a national resource and a monument to man and the mountains.

Appalachian mountain life of the 1800s returns through the interpretation of National Park Service staff members at Humpback Rocks in Virginia. Here at milepost 8, tourists discover living history as Lewis and Beth Wright, together with Dorval Banks (below), dress in authentic costumes and re-create log-cabin days. While the men perform such outside chores as feeding livestock, shaping wood for ax handles, and gathering kindling for the fireplace, Beth stirs up a noon meal. Behind her hang cast-iron pots and a three-legged frying pan called a "spider."

Highland romance: Candlelight mood in North Carolina's Great Craggies comes from a setting sun muted by moisture rising from forest leaves. The parkway magic inspires honeymooners Gary and Barbara Clark (far right).

FOLLOWING PAGES: *A piper's tune skirls high above the parkway on Grandfather Mountain in North Carolina. Each year descendants of Scots who came as settlers in the late 1740s gather on the mountain for songs, dances, and athletic games.*

Natchez Trace:
The South's Storied Route

By Christine Eckstrom Lee   Photographs by Steve Wall

Carved by centuries of wear from footstep, hoofbeat, and wagon wheel,
a still-traveled swale of the Old Natchez Trace sinks between banks of soft
soil—called loess—anchored by hardwood roots in southern Mississippi.

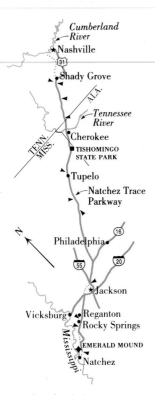

KILOMETERS	150
STATUTE MILES	100

Cumberland River

★Nashville

Shady Grove

Tennessee River

Cherokee

TISHOMINGO
STATE PARK

Tupelo

Natchez Trace
Parkway

Philadelphia

Jackson

Vicksburg   Reganton
Rocky Springs

EMERALD MOUND

Natchez

Arrowheads denote areas
of access to remnants
of Old Trace

Dotted line shows future
route of parkway

Throughout the South, memory runs old and long and deep, alive and fluid like the slow brown creeks that vein the land. It runs with insistence like the bark of the hounds that bay all night in the Mississippi woods. It lives in the people like a song mother sang, a lullaby hummed in idle moments; the tune is always there, running in the mind, sometimes unnamed, never forgotten.

One name evokes the course of this memory: the Natchez Trace, the fabled route that runs through the heart of the Deep South. Like southern life itself—deeply rooted in history but noticeably altered by progress—the name refers to two byways, the Old Trace and the New Trace. The first is a pioneer trail, the second is a modern parkway, and together they present two different faces of the land.

Haunting remnants of sinuous footpaths make up the broken network of trails collectively known as the Old Trace. Like the moon's hidden dark side, the vanishing route casts thoughts of shadowy nightmares as it winds through woodlands, swamps, and hills. It begins by the bluffs of the Mississippi River in Natchez, Mississippi, one of the oldest cities on the mighty waterway that flows from America's innermost reaches. The Old Trace cuts a deep swale in the Mississippi soil and makes a faint scar along the highland ridges of northwest Alabama and south-central Tennessee. It leads past fertile lowlands once carpeted by cotton, skirts hardscrabble patch farms in the red clay hills, and passes from the white pillared mansions of antebellum Mississippi to the plain frame houses tucked in the hollows of the Tennessee hills. In its geographical passage, the Old Trace covers 500 miles from Natchez to Nashville, where it ends downtown by the banks of the Cumberland River.

The side of the Trace most often seen and traveled is the Natchez Trace Parkway. Established in 1938, this clean-cut, two-lane, paved road leisurely follows the contours of the countryside for some 400 miles. The parkway commemorates the Old Trace, which dips in and out of sight of the present-day thoroughfare like a moving shadow, following in full view, then disappearing behind a tree in a thicket of grasping bushes and tangled vines. In sharp contrast the parkway stands in clear sight like the shiny plate of the summer moon. Wide grassy shoulders and beautiful stands of dogwoods, pines, oaks, and maples decorate the recreational federal road, which the National Park Service administers. Archaeological sites, historic landmarks, and signs along the parkway tell the story of the Old Trace.

On foot and by car, in the paintbrush season of autumn and in the sultry months of spring, I explored both worlds of this route. Throughout my journey I searched for the imprint that the Trace has left on the South.

No one remembers the bison. Legend holds that their hoofs pounded rough trails in the southern wilderness and that the Trace began as a route followed by the wandering herds. When the French settled at Natchez in 1716, the Old Trace existed as a network of Indian trails. It connected the Natchez tribe of southwest Mississippi with the Choctaw tribe of the state's interior and the Chickasaw tribe centered in the north near

Land of Two Traces: A network of paths trodden by prehistoric Indians, the Old Trace eventually became the overland connection between Nashville, Tennessee, and Natchez, Mississippi. Today, the modern 400-mile paved Natchez Trace Parkway commemorates the frontier route.

present-day Tupelo. From Chickasaw country, the Old Trace ran to the salt licks around Nashville, where several tribes shared the hunting ground. Even before the American Revolution, the Natchez Indians—like the buffalo—had disappeared from the region. Their memory, however, survives in the name of the city where their villages once stood and in the name of the rugged trail that began there.

The Old Trace, which coursed through a fearsome wild land full of bandits and Indians and "devils" in the swamps, was the only way home for the bold wayfarers who made it famous. They were Ohio Valley settlers known as "Kaintucks." In the early 1800s they floated down the Mississippi on flatboats. They sold their crops, goods—and boats—in Natchez or New Orleans, then walked or rode home over the notorious route. With gold stashed in their boot heels and sewn in their breeches, the Kaintucks stamped the Old Trace into a national road for thousands to follow.

Walking south, against the historic tide of the Kaintucks, I began my journey down the parkway on foot. (The word "trace" is from the Old French for "footpath.") Orange and gold leaves on the trees resembled flashing coins in the October breeze as I joined hiker David Crews in Tennessee. David, a native Mississippian, was walking the entire length of the Trace. For several days I hiked with him. We covered about 65 miles through highlands from southern Tennessee across Alabama into northern Mississippi. It was fitting that we shared the journey; Kaintuck boatmen usually banded together for safety during the trip up the Old Trace.

"I've wanted to hike the Natchez Trace for a long time," David explained. "I was raised in the shadow of the Trace, and my ancestors settled and developed much of this land. The parkway cuts across this region of the South geographically, socially, culturally, and historically. It's a splendid road, with great natural beauty."

Our days on the trail were full of conversations about the land and people of Natchez Trace country and the parkway with its lush setting of hardwoods and pines. The route is free of commercial billboards, and the air is country sweet. As we crossed into Alabama, the view opened over broad fields of cotton. The fluffy bolls, ready for picking, lined up in rows stark white against the red soil.

The Old Trace comes out after sundown. One particular night we walked until long after dark. Moonlight illuminated our path down a red clay road. The pleasant world of the parkway faded from mind, and the menacing world of the old paths loomed large. Distant hounds released mournful howls in the woods as we silently wound wide-eyed through the darkness of the black hills.

We camped among the tall pines. A low-slung moon and a sea of stars filled the sky, the stars winking between swaying branches. The forest came alive with the sounds of screech owls, screaming crickets, and unseen night creatures rustling in the trees and fallen leaves. I understood why the Mississippi woods have been the setting for so many legends of ghosts and strange beasts—mesmerizing tales told in a deep slow drawl with punch lines that snatch the breath away. I imagined all manner of danger. I lay awake, alert to the sorcery that lies dormant in the darkness and waits for an approaching footfall to open its mean red eye and bring it to life.

The Kaintuck boatmen were no less afraid of the wilderness. They usually had more to fear, however, from their fellow man than from the Trace's natural hazards, which included sucking swamps, flooding streams, insect swarms, snakes, bears, and panthers. The Old Trace was "infested with a gange of Banditti," wrote Tennessee's governor in 1803; vicious outlaws roamed the trails, robbing Kaintucks and other travelers and leaving no witnesses. The Kaintucks themselves were only a noose's length closer to the law than their murderous adversaries. Mark Twain once imagined a flatboatman's boast: "I'm the man they call Sudden Death and General Desolation! Sired by a hurricane, dam'd by an earthquake. . . . I split the everlasting rocks with my glance, and I quench the thunder when I speak! Whoo-oop! Stand back and give me room . . . for I'm about to turn myself loose!"

To celebrate their journey downriver and to fortify their spirits for the trek up the Trace, the boatmen usually turned themselves loose in Natchez-Under-the-Hill. This river stop was a hard-drinking, cardsharping, pistol-smoking town with the reddest set of lights on the Mississippi. It served as a landing for Natchez proper. The city spread out atop tall bluffs, looking across the river at the table-flat lowlands of Louisiana. Beneath the bluffs Natchez-Under-the-Hill, reclining on the Mississippi bank like a temptress, lured the Kaintuck boatmen ashore. If they survived the lusty nights spent Under-the-Hill, the boatmen set off into the wilds—with or without their gold—for the long trek north to Nashville.

Today, the wicked reputation of Natchez-Under-the-Hill has slipped into folklore, and most of the town has been swallowed by the river. Steep-sloped Silver Street still remains, however. Old brick buildings stand hip-to-shoulder along the street and descend single file to the Mississippi shore. I strolled the street's weathered wood sidewalks with ambling groups of visitors. Some had just stepped ashore from the riverboat *Delta Queen*, moored at the foot of Silver Street. One woman gazed up at a building as if to hear screams, shots, and unspeakable oaths of old. But the buildings now house shops, restaurants, a country inn, and one lone saloon where the plunky strumming of a banjo keeps the beat of the past.

Atop the bluffs, Natchez appeared sleepy in the warmth of spring. Old oaks shaded its checkerboard of streets, prim with 18th- and 19th-century homes. Set deep in the trees and gardens downtown and on rolling estates fringing the city stand the crown jewels of Natchez: the mansions of the Old South. Spacious and grand, they rise like Grecian temples in a dream world of tall white pillars and hot pink azaleas, long breezy galleries and Spanish moss streamers.

Many of the antebellum houses are still owned by descendants of the families who built them. Each spring and fall their doors are opened to visitors for a month of touring and celebration known as the Pilgrimage. Since 1932, the year of the first Natchez Pilgrimage, the idea has spread to communities throughout the South. In Natchez the house tour has become a major industry. It generates revenue for maintaining the old southern splendor of the homes.

During the spring pilgrimage, the lawns and gardens of Natchez are smothered in colorful blooms of irises, tulips, daffodils, and azaleas. The trees are twined with wisteria vines fragrant and heavy with lavender grape-bunch blossoms. Belles in hoopskirts welcome tourists inside the mansions that have names both stately and lyrical: Longwood, Dunleith, Rosalie. I delighted in details that preserve a sense of life long ago: a fainting couch, a petticoat mirror, a three-legged chair that lets a soldier sit comfortably while wearing his sword. At Longwood, the abrupt end of the era of fabulous wealth that built the mansions is plainly displayed. The house is unfinished; inside, old buckets, tools, and ladders lie where the workmen from the North left them suddenly to return home at the outbreak of the Civil War in April 1861.

The War Between the States wrecked the agrarian economy of the South. Many cities never fully recovered their antebellum glory. The mansions of Natchez became headquarters and hospitals for the Union Army. Memory of occupation, marches, and battles fought ever closer to home exists in visible expression: The polished cypress floors in the mansion called Rosalie still bear the scars of Union spurs.

Touring Natchez, I heard a poem set to music that spoke to the powerful sense of history and place that pervades life in the Deep South:

> Listen more often to things than beings
> 'Tis the ancestors' breath
> When the fire's voice is heard
> 'Tis the ancestors' breath
> In the voice of the waters. . . .

Voices of the past rise to a chorus here. Natchez is rich with the feeling of dark secrets and untold tales both heroic and tragic, of mysteries kept in small velvet boxes, never to be opened, but always remembered.

Most of the communities born of the Natchez Trace and the towns, farms, and people located near it lie concealed from view, just beyond the parkway's tunnel of trees. One such community is Reganton. This tiny crossroads town stands one mile from the parkway, south of Vicksburg and Jackson. I learned of Reganton from Bill Ferris, a folklife scholar, and director of the Center for the Study of Southern Culture at the University of Mississippi. "Reganton's whole history is tied to the Old Trace," he told me. During the Civil War, Grant's troops marched along the Trace nearby. They were en route to Jackson, which they burned, and Vicksburg, which they captured in a turning-point campaign of the war. Earlier, during the War of 1812, a few settlers in the Reganton area saw Andrew Jackson. His army of Tennessee volunteers trooped along the Trace and back—twice. The route was Jackson's warpath. The second time over it he returned home in triumph after defeating the British in the Battle of New Orleans.

"Now the Trace is a historical monument," Bill said. "The parkway symbolizes the passing of an era. But the Old Trace still weaves in and out of people's lives in Reganton. They have tales."

Mrs. Aden White shared her tales of the road. She lives in a white frame house beside the parkway, just east of Reganton. "Of course I'm almost as old as the Natchez Trace!" she said. "I grew up on the Old Trace. When I was a girl, we would climb the high banks and chase ground squirrels up there. We knew about the robbers. They were a very real thing to us, because it was in Rocky Springs, just down the road, where they were supposed to have gone into hibernation. We thought that if you

---

FOLLOWING PAGES: *Tupelo and bald cypress guard a swamp northeast of Jackson, Mississippi. Brutish outlaws lurked in such morasses and preyed on Trace travelers, sinking their victims' bodies into the murky waters.*

could just find the right place, where they robbed the travelers on the Trace, you could find the hidden loot.

"Once, in a pine grove, I found a brass U. S. Army teaspoon. It was cankered and old. At first I thought it was gold. My mother said, 'Well, that was probably left when the Yankees came through and camped there.' I've lost it now. It went the way of the spoons, I reckon."

Mrs. White took a long breath. "This land is my briar patch and my roots. There's an inside something that I just can't describe. But when I'm away for a while and I'm on my way back, something begins to swell in my heart and fill me up, and when I arrive here I know that it's home. No other place gives me that feeling."

Evidence of the earliest ones to call the Natchez Trace home dots the land along the length of the parkway. Ceremonial and burial mounds of the ancient Indians rise in clearings and in farmers' fields. The mounds are lush grassy domes, distinct but softened by the years. Near the parkway north of Natchez, I climbed to the top of Emerald Mound. Ancestors of the Natchez Indians built this massive seven-acre structure of earth. High up, the wind rushed in my ears like the sound of drums and thunder. I watched racing storm clouds darken and shift overhead, as if their changing patterns were an expression of the music of the skies.

By the mid-1700s, most of the Natchez Indians had been killed or sold into Caribbean slavery; some had fled to Chickasaw land to the north. Less than a century later, the Chickasaw and Choctaw were

Natchez fishermen Jim Morris (left) and Dusty Owen display three-pound buffalofish netted in Mississippi waters that yearly flood lowlands. Farmers grow crops in the ground left dry and silt-rich by the receding overflow.

marched west by federal troops to reservations in Oklahoma Territory. But a few Choctaws escaped the forced evacuation and remained in central Mississippi. Their descendants live close to the parkway near Philadelphia, northeast of Jackson, where they maintain a peaceful, private existence on a part of their ancestral homeland.

Choctaw traditional life has changed, but a handful of older men and women still practice the hallmark craft of basket weaving. At his home on a wooded hilltop northwest of Philadelphia, I visited Melvin Henry. In his 70s, he is the last of the Choctaw white-oak basket weavers.

Dressed in a visor cap and railroad-style striped bib overalls, Melvin greeted me under a big spreading white oak by his modest frame house. He was born in a log cabin that once stood on the hill, and his father taught him white-oak basketry under the old tree. Its canopy of shade is still Melvin's workshop.

I watched him shave long oak strips with a draw knife, making them thin and flexible enough to work. Melvin learned to make the baskets not as a craft for craft's sake, but as a necessary part of life.

"One year I grew a lot of corn," he said. "And I didn't have a basket for it, so I used a tub. I'm telling you that tub was unhandy. So I decided, well, I've got to have some baskets. I got me some timber, and I made some baskets. Then people found out and asked me, 'Where'd you get those new baskets?' I said, 'I made them.' And they said, 'How about making me some?' That's how it started."

He held up the smooth strip of wood, turning it in his hands. "People don't want to learn to make baskets anymore, but *o-o-o-wee!* They want them more than ever. I can't make enough baskets to fill all the requests. It takes time and hard work, but I'm enjoying it myself. But I'm the last, nobody but me. And I sure have a lot more baskets to make." I left him alone, beneath the old tree, shaping his next white-oak basket.

The extensive forests of the central Trace country provide white oaks for Melvin's baskets, pines for the region's huge timber industry, and a wonderful place to indulge in the rural South's pastime of coon hunting. A good coon dog, although expensive, is a loyal companion, a wonder in action, and a source of pride. And, many owners feel, after a bounding, barking lifetime of faithful service, a good coon dog should not simply go to his reward: He should be remembered. No other place does a better job of remembering than Coon Dog Cemetery. It nestles up in the hills and hollows near the Old Trace in Alabama.

At the West Colbert County Sportsman's Club near Cherokee, J. D. Tate told me the story behind the cemetery:

"Old Troop started it all. A man named Key Underwood had a real good coon dog that was raised back there in those hills. So when old Troop died, Key said, 'I'm going to bury him where he's always hunted, under his favorite tree.' That was back in 1937, and from that, everybody who had a coon dog buried him there. It's the only one in the world, I reckon."

On Labor Day at Coon Dog Cemetery, a big picnic is held. Musicians play, and the hundred graves are decorated with flowers. I asked if the cemetery was restricted to coon dogs.

"Oh yes," said a friend of Mr. Tate's. "Years ago, one man buried a squirrel dog out there. When they found out, they made him dig that dog up and move him."

Up in those hills, down a red dirt road at the crest of a ridge, a white sign with a drawing of a dog treeing a coon points to Coon Dog Cemetery. I wandered among the graves and marveled at the names: Banjo Bandit, Beanblossom Bommer, Crooked Oaks Ruby, and of course, Troop.

One grave had pawprints in the concrete marker; some stones had carvings of baying hounds treeing coons; some graves had snapshots and kennel club papers set under glass, and several had collars and tags pinned to wooden crosses or stumps. The resting place of Blue Kate bore written testimony to her prowess. Though lost in the line of duty, she had treed more than 200 coons in six years. The grave marker was signed by four witnesses. I liked Black Ranger's inscription: "He was good as the best and better than the rest." Surely no finer thing could be said about a good ole, rough-and-ready, fleet-footed, tongue-lollin', hard-yelpin', fun-lovin' coon dog.

From the shrine of Alabama's hound-dog country, the paved Trace crosses the Tennessee River and winds north through roller-coaster hills. At Shady Grove, Tennessee, the parkway ends where the Old Trace dissolves into a web of narrow local roads that curve past small towns and green pastures to Nashville. On the high south bank of the Cumberland River in the hub of the music city sits a reproduction of the humble log stockade called Fort Nashborough. It marks the traditional end of the Old Trace. The original fort was built in 1780, right before the first pioneers set off from Natchez on Indian trails and headed north homeward through

Modern antebellum dandies, Calvit (left) and Wade Ratcliffe play host in the Natchez Spring Pilgrimage, an open-house celebration of the Old South. "Confederate General" Jim Yarbrough greets guests at Rosalie mansion.

FOLLOWING PAGES: *Leafy hardwoods outline pastures and cornfields near Shady Grove, Tennessee, the northern end of the Natchez Trace Parkway.*

untamed lands. Amid the brick buildings and high rises, the little fort imparts a simple reminder of wilderness beginnings. The romance and intrigue of those early days inspired Eudora Welty, the distinguished novelist. One collection of her tales, *The Wide Net & Other Stories*, and a fantasy called *The Robber Bridegroom* are set along the Old Trace. She was relaxing at home after festivities honoring her 75th birthday when I visited her in Jackson, Mississippi.

"My stories reflect my feeling for the Natchez Trace more than anything else," she explained. "The whole idea fascinated me, the way the Trace linked the past. Between Natchez and the Tennessee line was nothing but canebrakes and wilderness and bears and Indians and unexplored land and everything.

"For the merchants who came down the river, before the time of the steamboat, and sold their goods, and got their bags of gold, the only way home was the Trace. It was the jungle. It was the forest primeval. So they went this perilous way.

"Life then seemed as dangerous as it is now. The bandits were hovering overhead, and the Indians were coming up from the river, and everybody was lurking, and the bears were getting ready to chew them up, and everybody wanted their gold, except the bears I guess.

"Lorenzo Dow from New England was wandering around on the Trace saving souls, and John James Audubon was wandering around painting birds—it was just so unbelievably full of life and very romantic and very dangerous and brave."

Lorenzo Dow was one of the first of many circuit-riding preachers who traveled the Trace and inspired the wilderness settlers with fiery words of faith. Eudora Welty pictured a scene with the evangelist: "You know how mad he was. He would come riding down the Trace through the wilderness, and people would be watching for him in a clearing with torches burning. Everybody would be gathered into a circle of firelight, and he would clatter up on his horse saying something about God and Divine Love. And they used to hire little black boys and little Indian boys to climb up in the trees, so that when they saw him coming they could start blowing on trumpets like angels. That must have been so exciting!"

Her eyes glistened as she talked, her voice soft and gracious. "The Old Trace gives you a feeling of what has been," she said. "It's very evocative of danger and the loneliness of travel." She paused, collected a thought, then said: "I really do have a belief in the reality of place. There's something in there that endures, something emanates from a place. Under and over all the cement of the parkway, I feel like the Old Natchez Trace is still there."

For the casual traveler the faraway times of the historic route may seem as unreal and elusive as the worn path that cuts deep in the soil of the woodlands and then fades from sight beneath a carpet of leaves. But the Old Trace is the past and a presence, there for those who will find it and real to those who remember.

"After I was married in 1933, my husband brought me to Tennessee," remembers Gladys Sherill. "I loved the land. We sharecropped ... raised corn and hay and six children. I have it all written down in the record, my Bible."

"As a youngster, I heard the wagons full of cured meats a-rumblin' over the Trace up on that sunset ridge," says H. C. Meacham, a sheep farmer in the Franklin, Tennessee, area. The Old Trace crosses the fields of James Berry (opposite) in south-central Tennessee. "I've heard that Andrew Jackson came through here. My granddad said that people in his day set up stands on the Trace and sold vegetables and other things. But that was before it was paved. People come from all over to see it, but it's just for pleasure ridin' now."

Energetic cyclists pump up a winding grade in Tishomingo State Park. The Natchez Trace Parkway bisects this woodland retreat developed in northeastern Mississippi by the Civilian Conservation Corps in the late 1930s. In the blight of the Depression the CCC brought the state park system into bloom. April sunlight at Tishomingo highlights oak and beech (right) and warms a fire-pink catchfly (below).

FOLLOWING PAGES: *Mist from a spillway showers eastern redbud, one of Tishomingo's first splashes of spring color.*

Great River Road:
Beside the Mississippi

By Cynthia Russ Ramsay   Photographs by Terry Eiler

Irresistible roadside attraction, the Mississippi River channels grain barges between Lansing, Iowa, and the far Wisconsin shore. Water traffic often pulls sightseers from a nearby shoreline drive called the Great River Road.

In the blackness and suffocating heat the drum boomed a slow, steady rhythm as elder Amos Owen sang the praises of Wakan-Tanka, the one Great Spirit and the creator of all that is. The songs also summoned the lesser spirits, which have many forms and reside in all things. More water was dribbled on the heated stones, and steam hissed up from the pit in the earthen floor of the Indian sweat lodge. Then Amos, a respected and renowned religious leader, chanted a prayer in the guttural tones of the Sioux language.

The purification rite had begun earlier in the evening with offerings of tobacco. While the stones were heating in the bonfire each participant wrapped pinches of tobacco in bits of red cloth, linking them together with thread. Taking the tobacco ties with us, we crept into the low, dome-shaped, tarpaulin lodge. Inside, the sacred pipe was passed around our circle of eight, for according to the lore of the Sioux, Wakan-Tanka and his intermediaries will listen to all who smoke in a holy ceremony. But to be heard and to commune with the supernatural, one must also be spiritually prepared—cleansed in body and spirit by the ritual sweat bath.

The cycle of songs and prayers had started when the first seven stones were brought in. It was repeated three times more, until 21 rocks lay in the pit, and the heat seemed more than I could bear. Still we sat, until one by one each worshiper, drenched in sweat, voiced his own fervent prayer. With that emotional crescendo, the two-hour ritual came to an end, and we filed out of the lodge and stood quietly in the wonderfully chill Minnesota night.

This encounter with the ancient religion of the Sioux was one of many memorable experiences I had during a journey along a segment of the Great River Road. For most of its length, this route is actually twin highways. Curving through the Canadian provinces of Manitoba and Ontario, the road enters the U.S. at two points in Minnesota: International Falls and the Roseau area. Near the source of the Mississippi at Lake Itasca, the road stretches its two arms along parallel banks that embrace the picturesque heart of the route, the river itself. About 100 different route numbers identify various stretches of the Great River Road as it follows the Mississippi through ten states to the Gulf of Mexico. With lanes totaling almost 5,000 miles as they trace both sides of the river, the course ranks as one of the world's longest scenic highways.

From the 534-acre Prairie Island Sioux Community outside Red Wing, Minnesota, I headed south. The Great River Road's emblem, a green-and-white pilot wheel, served as my constant guide. Crossing and recrossing the bridges to Wisconsin and Illinois, I would drive both sides of the Mississippi River before my journey ended in the tranquil village of Bellevue, Iowa, 230 miles south of Red Wing.

The dual road led me through the long, verdant valley of the Upper Mississippi. The valley rarely extends more than four miles wide. Wooded bluffs bracketing the narrow corridor have kept their rugged contours because they were left untouched by the last Ice Age glacier, which leveled areas of the upper Midwest. I lingered in cameo river towns,

From Canada to the Gulf of Mexico, the Great River Road serves ten states; the author visited the four at left. The route's lanes run simultaneously on both sides of the Mississippi, aiding travelers seeking cozy waterfront towns and sportsmen hankering for quiet wetlands with abundant wild game.

dominated by church steeples and waterfront parks, and I toured small cities such as La Crosse, Wisconsin, and Dubuque, Iowa. Between the towns, I passed miles of wooded bottomlands that form part of the Upper Mississippi River National Wildlife and Fish Refuge. Sometimes I would pull off the highway to find a fringe of forest and backwater still unmarred by development and still the haunt of muskrats, white-tailed deer, and turtles dozing on logs. Multitudes of ducks, herons, and egrets nest there. Millions more, including Canada geese and tundra swans, funnel along the Mississippi flyway during the spring and fall migrations.

Like the millions of people who come to vacation here annually and the many who live in this farming region, I was drawn again and again to the river. Its mirror-smooth sloughs twisted among islets overgrown with trees; its marshes teemed with waterfowl, and its backwaters were so overgrown with water lilies that almost no open water remained. No less fascinating was watching navigation on the looping main channel. Tiny towboats pushing cumbersome barges looked like ants moving loaves of bread past vacationers' houseboats and outboards.

One resident lured to the region is lawyer Philip Gartner, a lean, tanned outdoorsman. He resides in Lake City and lives to go sailing on the broad expanse of the Mississippi known as Lake Pepin. As the wind heeled the *Sonata* over hard and his 26-foot Pearson fairly flew across the water's sparkling pinpoints of sunlight, Philip told me why he has turned down lucrative job offers in larger towns.

"I've traded money for a terrific life-style. Tricky gusty winds make this the best sailing in the Midwest south of Lake Superior. From April to October I can go sailing on my lunch hour. The sloughs just south of here offer duck hunting in the fall, and some of the bluffs slope down in ski runs in the winter. Most of the year I can sit in my car and watch bald eagles swoop down from the ridges to fish."

With boating, waterskiing, swimming from the beaches, camping in the summer, and ice fishing in the winter, tourism has become Lake City's fastest-growing industry. Other changes have taken place as well.

Holding the sails trimmed flat for a swift crossing to Pepin, Wisconsin, Philip talked about the pollution that has killed the lake's commercial fishing. Some 25 miles long, Lake Pepin owes its existence to the rushing Chippewa River, which deposits sand at its confluence with the Mississippi. This debris forms a natural dam that creates the lake upstream. The slack waters act as a settling pond that purifies the river below but taints the lake with such industrial poisons as PCBs. In 1975, state authorities warned that some of the lake fish were contaminated and unsafe for humans to eat more than once a week.

Nothing, however, has marred the view of Pepin, tucked prettily under a green brow of bluffs that flared with a few gold and scarlet leaves tinted by September frosts. We docked at the marina in time for lunch at the Harbor View Cafe. Gourmet food draws an enthusiastic clientele, some of whom drive many miles on the Great River Road to get here.

"We have no secret recipes. We just use butter instead of margarine, bake our own bread, and serve fresh fish and vegetables," explained cook Judy Krohn. She had grown the squash for the soup featured that day. Judy and the owners of the restaurant, all refugees from big cities, were seeking more than an income when they settled here. They were looking for the means to a quiet, simple life.

There has been a steady trickle of urban people into southwest

Wisconsin. This rural corner north of La Crosse is less developed for recreation than the Minnesota side, so real estate prices for old, abandoned farm buildings are relatively low. Jobs, however, are in short supply, and newcomers must create their own opportunities. Judy's husband, Gib, fashions ceramic whistles in the shape of animals and boats. He also works in construction and commercial fishing, or at whatever job he can get. His whistles are sold by the Red Balloon Gallery, which opened in 1982 in the drowsy hamlet of Stockholm.

To visit Mark and Carol Edwards, the young couple who own the gallery, I drove north from Pepin. The Great River Road followed the scalloped shoreline. Every turn brought a new vista of shining water and forested shore. Ahead the procession of bluffs crested and dipped with a languorous regularity. The occasional bald shoulders of limestone breaking the mantle of vegetation suggested the massive walls of an old fortress.

"Stockholm is a comfortable place to make a small income stretch," Mark told me at the gallery. "We've learned to live on very little by cutting our own wood for heat, doing our own plumbing, patching everything together ourselves." He guided me among the paintings, pottery, and sculpture of two dozen artists, nearly all newcomers to the area.

The first immigrants to the Upper Mississippi came for beaver and other animal pelts in the early 1700s, and many towns began as fur trading posts. By the 1830s, timber brought bigger profits than fur. Armies of lumberjacks cut into the great forests along the streams that feed the Mississippi's tributaries. At Beef Slough, once a channel of the Chippewa just south of Pepin, logs that had come bucking down the fast-flowing

Polished elegance brightens the dining room of the Villa Louis, an 1870 mansion (opposite) in Prairie du Chien, Wisconsin. Trappers and traders swaggering to market with furs and buckskins brought the town prosperity.

PRECEDING PAGES: *In southern Minnesota, October moisture veils the Great River Road and maple-basswood forests on the Mississippi's western shore.*

river were herded into rafts more than 1,000 feet long and floated to saw-mills downstream. Passing Beef Slough on my way back south on the Great River Road, I saw no traces of the human enterprise that moved millions of dollars' worth of timber downstream. The quiet waters had re-verted to long-legged wading birds, such as great blue herons and egrets.

The last lumber raft was towed down the Mississippi in 1915. Steam-boats plied the waters a little longer, and towns like Fountain City, Wis-consin, supplied fuel. Retired riverboat pilot Allen Fiedler remembers people sitting by their woodpiles on the riverbank waiting to make a sale. "In the old days, the river was ornery and unpredictable. It could be a mile wide and just inches deep, then suddenly it could become inches wide and a mile deep. The Corps of Engineers was dredging, trying to maintain a six-foot channel, but there wasn't six feet on most of the river."

Only the old stern-wheelers—capable, they say, of running on heavy dew—could safely negotiate the waters. Up until the 1930s, Mark Twain had been right when he scoffed at efforts to control the river: ". . . might as well bully the comets in their courses . . . as to try to bully the Mississippi into right and reasonable conduct." For years the Army

Engineers had been removing snags. "Pulling the river's teeth," Twain called it. Wing dams, made from brush and rocks submerged in place, helped move the water into navigation channels, but the river remained an obstacle course of shoals and sandbars and sunken debris.

Then in the 1930s the corps built 25 locks and dams between Minneapolis and St. Louis. With the river's free flow halted and with constant dredging to hold the nine-foot navigation channel, the river was finally tamed. The impounded river flooded bottomlands, creating tens of thousands of acres of marshes and shallows that shelter millions of migratory ducks, geese, swans, and coots.

These wetlands are heaven to sportsmen, and the Great River Road is a major passage to the hunting grounds of the Upper Mississippi Refuge. On October 1, opening day of duck season,   *(Continued on page 89)*

Great River Road hangout thrives on St. Feriole Island in Prairie du Chien. In 1965, when the Mississippi crested at 25 feet, the bar flooded; the owner's daughter had to don hip boots and wade in to rescue the cash register.

*Cork-line of a seine net snakes past Mike Sorensen on the Upper Mississippi.
The last commercial seiner in his family, he sells his catch—mainly carp
and buffalofish—through a firm that his grandfather started in Bay City,
Wisconsin. Hurrying toward Mississippi backwaters, duck hunters (opposite)
carry the marsh grass they will use to camouflage their boat.*

Becalmed on the edge of a lotus
bed, anglers go after sunfish
in the sweltering backwaters of
the Mississippi. Another skilled
fisher, a great blue heron
(above) lifts off from a stump
field, a bottomland forest
clear-cut years ago and
swamped when dams backed
up the mighty river.

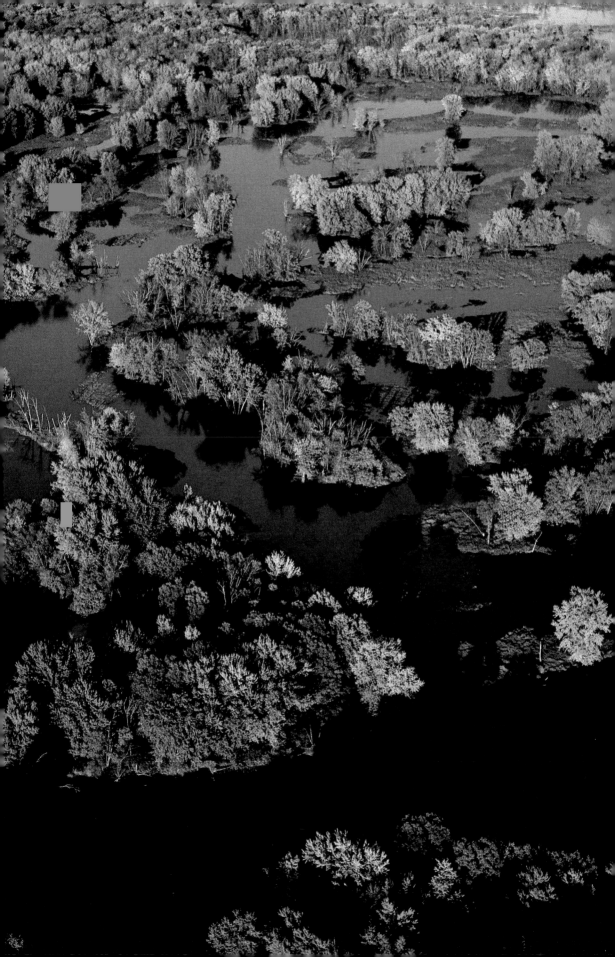

I traveled south on the Great River Road to Trempealeau, Wisconsin. I had decided to try my hand at duck hunting with Ray Walters, as competent a shooting instructor as any beginner could want. I had visions of slogging through misty marshes at the first gray light of dawn. Instead I found myself with Ray scanning the robin's egg-blue sky of mid-morning from our natural blind on a shrubby islet. I was sweating only slightly in my camouflage jacket and cap. On one side two dozen decoys gently bobbed 30 yards offshore. On the more stagnant waters, patches of duckweed floated in a broad green layer, flat as miniature tiles on the black water. The size of a kernel of wheat, the duckweed didn't look like much of a plant. But each tiny clump had its own system of root hairs and provided food for the birds we so earnestly sought.

In the hour before the legal starting time Ray went over the basics of shooting on the wing. "The best shots are 25 to 35 yards out; beginners make the mistake of shooting before the ducks are in range. Wait to see the ring around the duck's eyes before firing." A ragged barrage marked the noon opening. Shooting started downstream; then a flock of pintails sweeping north drew fire from clusters of hunters all along the way. A couple of blue-winged teal turned toward us.

"Take 'em," Ray ordered.

Before I could hoist my 12-gauge the birds had flashed by.

Some mallards were heading our way in a tight wedge formation.

"Now," Ray whispered.

I fired as fast as I could, pumping the gun for a second shot. The mallards sailed safely by.

"You were behind the birds before you started," Ray lectured. "You must swing the muzzle ahead of the target, and make sure you keep the gun moving."

Hunting regulations allow only three shells in the gun at a time. I never fired more than two, slowed in part by the recoil that kicked me in the jaw at every shot.

Ray could not let an opportunity go by much longer. He quickly bagged a pair of teal, each officially assigned 10 points in the 100-point daily limit set by state law.

"The birds were high, but I thought I ought to get those rusty shells out of the chamber," Ray said with a wink.

By 2 p.m. the opening flurry of activity had ended. The ducks seemed to have evaporated in the heat. Only sulphur butterflies flew weightlessly above the water. Any waterfowler knows that good weather makes for poor hunting. Wind stirs the ducks out of their resting places, and low temperatures make the birds nervous so that they fly around a lot. The warm spell had virtually halted the migration from the north.

At 4 o'clock some blue-winged teal angled overhead. Then a small V of ringnecks came into view. The birds were beginning to move again. Ray seemed determined that I get a duck. Of course he considered it unsportsmanlike to ground-swat the birds, yet he was frustrated by my

Wooded maze of wetlands sprawls outside La Crosse, Wisconsin. Locks and dams tamed the Mississippi in the 1930s. Impounded waters flooded nearly 200 square miles of forest and meadows and created an aquatic wonderland.

ineptitude. When a lone duck settled down among the decoys, Ray said: "I'll let out a hoot, and you take her when she jumps."

He hooted. The bird jumped. But I didn't shoot. In the johnboat on the way back, Ray agreed that even though I hadn't drawn a feather, I'd sure scared a lot of birds. The kidding about shots made and missed heightened the camaraderie that's so much a part of this sport.

The light was seeping out of the sky, forcing Ray to slow down as he maneuvered the boat around the sandbars and shallows.

"Twenty years ago we water-skied here. Now I have a hard time getting a boat through," he said. "I wouldn't be surprised if we're planting corn in this bay soon."

The specter of silt turning the Upper Mississippi into little more than a navigational ditch haunts many who live and play along the river. Cal Fremling, a professor of aquatic biology at Winona State University in Minnesota, estimates that the life expectancy of many marshes and lakes is 50 to 100 years. "These beautiful wetlands are a temporary thing. The dams that created them have slowed the river, so it can no longer flush the sediments downstream. The backwaters are filling in, while no new ones are being created," Cal told me in Winona.

I had arrived in Winona on a Tuesday, crossing the bridge onto the Minnesota side of the Great River Road. I climbed into a canoe with Cal, and we paddled out across a marshy expanse. A vigorous, athletic scholar, Cal never tires of the tranquillity of the backwaters. Indeed, the lazy current and calm seemed to unclutter my mind. I found myself absorbed in the small world around me. Whirligig beetles with oversize eyes scooted in tiny arcs on the surface film of the water. A great blue heron stretched its long neck forward for a stately takeoff. Ahead, several hundred coots attempting to lift off pattered and splashed across the water, their wings beating madly until the birds finally took flight.

We glided under cottonwood branches that splintered the sunlight into wavering shafts. Rounding a bend, we came to one of the hundreds of islands fringed by pale crescents of beach. Built from sand deposited by dredging operations of the Corps of Engineers, these beaches are the playgrounds of the river. Tons of dredge spoil had also been dumped in the wetlands. State officials and environmental groups protested, and the corps stopped using the backwaters as disposal sites.

But other abuses continue. Towboats with their big propellers stir up bottom sediments, Cal said, and large pleasure boats create wakes that scour away the riverbanks. A large amount of the fine silt wafts into the backwaters and settles. Another culprit threatening to choke off the wetlands is dirt eroded from hillside farms, which may lose as much as 20 tons of topsoil per acre each year.

Not many miles south of Winona, a bridge switched me back to the Wisconsin side of the Great River Road just outside La Crosse. More than 150,000 merrymakers had gathered for some good times of their own. Since 1961 the city has been the site of an Oktoberfest—a county fair with polka bands, bratwurst, and beer for a German flavor. Each year thousands of visitors throughout the Midwest attend this festival of parades, sports events, arts-and-crafts exhibits, and beer halls. The Oktoberfest generates about six million dollars in business annually.

In the 1850s La Crosse was one of the major ferry crossings for the wagon trains lumbering west. The city continued to grow and diversify, and today its citizens feel that it's got everything larger cities have except traffic jams. On the other hand, many Wisconsin towns lying to the south —DeSoto, Ferryville, Lynxville—barely survive. Their lifeline is the river at their doorstep and the customers it brings to the local bait-and-tackle shops, filling stations, and bars.

The Great River Road led me south past towns with weathered frame buildings that blended with the striking colors of autumn; on my right a gray mist lay on the dark river water, silhouetting fishermen in small boats anchored just offshore. There are 139 species of fish and 40 species of clams in the Upper Mississippi. Clamming was once a flourishing industry, and many river towns in Wisconsin and Iowa had a factory that cut pearl buttons from the shells. But plastic "pearl" buttons flooded the market in the 1950s and put them all out of business. About 20 years ago, clamming made a comeback when the Japanese began buying pellets made from the shells and using them as the nuclei for cultured pearls.

The clamming season was over by the time I arrived in Prairie du Chien, Wisconsin, in early October. The river was too cold for divers, and the current was too slow for traditional clam boats, explained Don Lessard, a burly kingpin of clamming on the Upper Mississippi. "Vibration from a motor closes up the clams, so we use a canvas mule. That's an underwater sail. It catches the current and pulls the boat and brail slowly downstream," he explained. The brail is a long bar that dangles hundreds of hooks from a series of chains. At a touch the clams instinctively clamp on the hooks and hang there even when the brail is hoisted out of the water.

Prairie du Chien is especially proud of its past as a prosperous fur center and, I discovered, is aggressively preparing for the future by dredging a big new port. The town's long history began when French explorers Louis Jolliet and Father Jacques Marquette, lured by legends of the great river of the West, canoed down the Wisconsin to its mouth. In 1673 they became the first white men to reach the Upper Mississippi.

When the Europeans arrived, they encountered the Fox, Sauk, and Winnebago Indians. Other cultures—of earlier Indians who built effigy mounds in the area—had disappeared. They left only their mysterious earthworks behind. These enigmatic remains lie in Effigy Mounds National Monument across the river near Marquette, Iowa.

"We've got a lot to learn about these mounds," National Park Service archaeologist Robert Petersen said as we hiked toward them. "We don't know what they were used for or why some contain burials and others are completely empty. We're beginning to think the mounds may have been a device to bring people together—an occasion to arrange marriages and allocate hunting grounds, for instance."

Some of the mounds take the form of bears or birds; others are shaped like domes. They range in length from 75 feet to 227 feet. When we came to Little Bear Mound, I paused for a while and studied its long, hump-shaped animal profile. So much effort had been required to move all that earth with only clamshells, digging sticks, and baskets. I was dismayed that the centuries have left so few clues to explain why.

The past speaks with a clear, bold voice in Galena, Illinois. The town's hilly, tree-shaded streets, its gingerbread mansions, its stately buildings with cupolas and fluted columns show little change since the days when local tycoons earned their riches trading in lead from the area's mines. Main Street still has the century-old stores, warehouses, and hotel built when Galena was a booming port with several breweries. Their beer, it is said, never left town.

Galena's fortunes declined when the demand for lead fell off and railroads upstaged steamboats, all but killing business on the town docks. Many people moved away, and for almost a hundred years Galena slumbered. Poverty kept the town in the 19th century. But in the 1960s, when small-town charm became marketable, Galena was able to trade on the wave of nostalgia that made people yearn for the way America used to be. Increasing numbers of visitors toured the town's restored homes and supported the local museums, which have grown to the astonishing number of 12. Among them is the Old General Store, featuring bolts of cloth, lanterns, and other wares of the 1800s. For sightseers eager to buy, the town offers more than 30 antique and gift shops. Their merchandise ranges from rag dolls and Icelandic woolens to sachets and English bone china.

Before I crossed the bridge to Galena, I had driven through miles of Iowa's rolling farm country that edges the river's bluffs. Silos towering from the fields marked the homes of hardworking, religious people who honor the virtues of thrift and self-sufficiency. I had seen them at the feed stores, where they talk of tractors, the price of hogs, and rising costs.

Gordon and Virginia Hartbecke, a spare middle-aged couple, have 55 Holsteins on their 300-acre farm northeast of Sherrill. They also raise some hogs, veal calves, and enough corn, oats, and alfalfa to feed their livestock. I was invited to visit them as long as I came before milking time. Their cows, Gordon told me, become uneasy around strangers and would give less milk.

The Hartbeckes do everything themselves—from baling hay to cleaning the stalls in the barn. And they buy only what they can pay cash for. "I've never owned a new tractor, new car or truck, but whatever I have is all paid for," Gordon said. Sometimes the Hartbeckes begin to tire of the never-ending chores and the 14 hours of work every day of the year. "Then I drive down the street in Dubuque, where some houses are three feet from each other, and I'm glad to be back." Gordon kept his eyes on the cows gathering near the barn. "They know it's milking time."

It was also time to leave and to continue on south toward Bellevue, the end of my journey. By now the season in Iowa had brushed all but the oaks with autumn color. Sharp winds hinted of the hard winter to come.

I left the Great River Road in Bellevue and parked on a hilltop for a parting look at the Mississippi, the mighty stream that lay at the heart of my journey. I had come to know it as an artery of commerce and as an avenue crowded with history. I had seen it as a playground, and I had found it to be a place where people scrabble to earn their livelihood. Yet, in spite of the towns and cities and all the activity along the Great River Road, the Upper Mississippi had retained a sense of wilderness. I hoped it would always remain that way.

Pre-Civil War pharmacy in Illinois now prescribes ice cream sodas. The renovated 1850s building fronts Main Street in Galena, once a lead mining center and home to the future President Ulysses S. Grant.

FOLLOWING PAGES: *Passing Marquette, Iowa, the* Delta Queen *revives the 1850s, when Mississippi steamboats became "palaces on paddlewheels."*

Nebraska 2:
Along Prairie Trails

By Gene S. Stuart   Photographs by Terry Eiler

"If you're a rancher in tallgrass country, you're never out of work," says LeRoy Louden, mending fence near Highway 2 in Nebraska. The state's roads shadow prairie trails traced years ago by self-reliant homesteaders.

The family stood in a cold meadow and stared out of the photograph and into the future. I gazed at them as openly, for through them I could see into the past. I was in Grand Island, Nebraska, at the Stuhr Museum of the Prairie Pioneer, where an exhibit of photographs preserves those times when trails of hope led westward toward hardship.

Time and progress have eased many of the privations and have blurred the old trails. But along a modern course, Nebraska Route 2, people and places repeatedly drew my thoughts back to that dramatic family photograph and its stark portrayal of pioneer life.

The bearded man in the picture faced the camera boldly; his wide shoulders, loose jacket, and heavy boots added a square, sturdy aspect. Two thin children at his side ventured a pinched, bewildered look. The woman's skirts brushed winter grasses; a dark hat framed a vulnerable face half turned away. She clutched a bundled infant, and her eyes telegraphed suffering. The family stood as solemn as stone around a tiny grave of a child. To that stern man and grieving woman, death was not defeat, but increased challenge. In pioneers you find people with determination and vision, people who shape the future in fantasy and strive to wrest a brighter reality from dreams.

In 1857 one group of visionaries staked their fortunes along the Platte River, founding Grand Island on the gamble that the area would become a major continental railroad center and they in turn would make their "everlasting fortunes." That grandiose dream did not materialize, but a practical vision did. Grand Island began to grow and prosper, for it lay close to westward-reaching trails, including the California-Oregon, the Oxbow, the Mormon, and the Nebraska City.

In the Stuhr Museum, historian Robert Manley told me about the old routes that have become Highway 2.

"Beginning east of here, at the Missouri River, the Old Freighters' Trail meandered from Nebraska City to Fort Kearny," he said. "In 1862 General J. R. Brown decided to pull freight over it with a wood-burning steam wagon. They got about four miles west of Nebraska City and broke down. Brown's idea was possible, though flawed. What were they going to use for fuel out on the treeless prairie?

"The plan did stimulate an interest for a more direct route to Fort Kearny. A surveyor, the story goes, marked a new route by turning over one furrow across the prairie with a team of mules and a plow. That was the beginning of Highway 2 east of here. Wagons just straddled that

---

Civilization intrudes lightly where Nebraska Route 2 slices through the grassy ranchland of the Sand Hills. Westward, motorists pass deep canyons and the tall bluffs of Pine Ridge country, the northern rim of the High Plains.

98

furrow and followed it. It had many names: the Old Freighters' Trail, Steamwagon Road, the Nebraska City Cutoff."

Northwestward from Grand Island the original route was a zigzag dirt road. It followed property lines marked by fenced fields and pastures on farms and ranches in the Sand Hills. The road passed through Pine Ridge country before ending at the South Dakota border. "To cross the Sand Hills, travelers had to stop and open more than 90 fence gates," Bob chuckled. He had told me how much he enjoys traveling the route. "A highway into the west to me is a thoroughfare of fantasy," he said. "What's at the end of that western road? Where's it going? I'll bet that my wife and I have been on that road dozens of times. Every time we get on Highway 2 and head that way we feel like saying: 'Do you feel the freedom?' "

I certainly did as I struck northwestward in the prime of autumn, a pioneer in my own travels, for Nebraska was new territory to me. My plan was to trace Highway 2 from Grand Island some 350 miles across plains and sandy hills and into Pine Ridge country. The road actually begins in Nebraska City on the Missouri River, but Interstate 80 now obliterates most of the original highway east of Grand Island. To the west the crooked course of old State 2 has been smoothed to a more direct two-lane road that quickly finds the Burlington Northern Railroad tracks and parallels them across the Sand Hills.

It was this rail line, completed in 1888, that gave birth to the western part of Highway 2 and a chain of towns evenly spaced like jeweled links along it. Railroaders named them, but not all survived. The towns that did still bear names of company employees, places in other states, and sometimes foreign locales—such as Cairo and Ravenna.

In Cairo, with its water tower and grain elevator soaring like royal monuments, I found sandy streets bearing Egyptian names: Nubia, Thebes, Alexandria. Would I find echoes of Italy's notable architecture and the famed Byzantine mosaics in Ravenna? In a sense I did. I found deep-verandaed Victorian houses and a business district where attached facades from a century ago knitted cafe to clothier, bar to barrister. And surrounding Ravenna were prairie-field mosaics: the green of sprouted winter wheat, the brown of plowed fields, the gold of hay and corn.

This region's fertile plains are part of the nation's breadbasket, but early explorers held another picture. They lamented this "useless" land between the Missouri River and the Rocky Mountains. Until the 1850s, many maps labeled this area The Great American Desert—Unexplored. Settlement and modern technology proved otherwise.

"The western two-thirds of Nebraska overlies the Ogallala Aquifer, the greatest natural underground water system in the United States." Speaking was Bill Pedersen, a county agricultural extension agent. I had met him in Broken Bow, the geographic center of Nebraska. "Water here is as important as oil is in other areas," Bill said. "Pivot irrigation came into this area about 15 years ago. It changed us from ranchers to farmers."

During my journey on the plains I had seen the irrigation system. Its giant rotating metal arms can squirt water as far as 2,600 feet, scattering moisture a circular mile. Most ranchers, however, still use the traditional windmill to pump water. One Saturday morning, nostalgia for the antique windmills of the 19th and 20th centuries drew collectors from as far away as Texas and New Jersey to an auction house in Broken Bow. I joined the excited crowd. Two complete mills with wooden blades lay dismantled before us. "There's three more out back," the auctioneer called out. We gazed at a display of extra parts: wooden blades, metal shafts, gears. There were also cast-iron figures. Designed to sit behind the mill blades as ornament and counterbalance, the figures depicted bulls, prancing horses, striding white roosters, and a fat brown squirrel. I could not stop admiring the squirrel, a splendid piece of American folk art. I resolved to bid as high as $50 for it.

"There were many different makes of windmills in the old days—just like the early days of automobiles," a man beside me said. "There were maybe over one hundred different brands. Many of them went out of business, just like the car companies did. Those are the rare ones now. I've got three kinds of old Dempsters, a 1, 4, and a 9. They don't make those any more, and they're hard to find."

Rare and enviable, evidently; a man in front of us turned to give my companion an admiring look. Throughout the day the auctioneer sang out. Eager hands shot up. By sundown one complete windmill had sold for more than $2,500. And the charming squirrel? It turned out to be far more valuable than I had dreamed. One man had admired it $2,600's worth.

After the auction, Bill Pedersen's wife, Corrinne, routed me past the Pedersens' willow tree ("Said to be Nebraska's largest weeping willow"). She reminded me that Arbor Day, a half-forgotten national celebration dedicated to tree planting, was founded in Nebraska. The event first took place in 1872; the state still observes it as a legal holiday on April 22.

Broken Bow's name stems from an Indian's hunting bow found shattered near a dugout that served as the settlement's first post office. My notion that dugouts belonged to the pioneer past was quickly dispelled when Corrinne guided me down one of the quiet neighborhood streets. There, on a corner, stood a roomy house with a stone facade. The entire dwelling reached far back into a hill. As with its primitive dugout prototype, the thick layer of natural-earth insulation keeps the house cool in summer and warm in winter. The owners had erected a sign in front proclaiming it The Little Prairie On the House.

"It fits right in with the traditional houses on this street," Corrinne said. "But it is a shock in summer to see the owners on top mowing the lawn on the roof."

Her comment brought to mind the story of an earlier hillside dugout with a grassy roof, the type that covered the houses inhabited by many Nebraska pioneers. A cold October night in 1859 had driven four hunters to seek shelter in the dugout of Henry Peck, his wife, and their 12 children on Wood River in central Nebraska. Cottonwood rafters overlaid with willow branches supported the structure's roof, forming an extension of the prairie-grass slopes where the farm animals roamed. The underground house stayed very warm in winter; with all ventilation shut off, the air inside was almost suffocating. But warm, stale air was much better than an icy night wind, and any lodging was welcome. As soon as the visitors had seated themselves at the table for the evening meal, Mr. Peck began to give thanks at great length. One of the hunters, William Stolley, recalled:

"Exhausted as we all were, the sultry air which was filled with all kinds of vapors began to make me drowsy during the prolonged prayer. Suddenly the roof . . . began to crack over our heads, becoming worse and worse, and in a few moments large quantities of dirt and litter came falling down upon us and our meal. The next moment a large ox broke through the roof with all four feet, but remained hanging with his belly across one of the rafters, bellowing piteously.

"Our 'cave father' was naturally wholly enraged, and stared at the ceiling. When the ox had settled down so that he was kicking with all four feet above the table, the fellow who was still praying, clenched his fist, which he shook threateningly at the unfortunate ox, and thundered a mighty 'God damn you!' Our meal, of course, was done for."

From Broken Bow, Highway 2 heads westward and enters the Sand Hills. The grassy dunes spread across one-quarter of the state. The largest dune area in the Western Hemisphere, the Sand Hills cover some 19,000 square miles and have often been called a sea of grass. My car eased along as quiet as a boat under sail, lifting and gently descending from one crest of highway to the next. Mile after mile I glided with no sound save the wind, the sight of it manifest in billowing waves of grass. In places plumes of sand rose as wind gnawed hillside spots into deep blowouts. Fat cattle stood belly deep in pasture. New-mown meadows held winter feed—bales of hay, some rectangular or rolled like shredded wheat, others rounded like huge loaves of bread.

I was deep in ranch country, and the people I met along Highway 2, usually cowboys in pickup trucks, lifted a forefinger from the steering wheel in a windshield wiper of a wave, or touched the wide brim of their hats and smiled, as neighborly to strangers as to their own kin. I braked for tumbleweed bounding across the highway and snakes slithering toward warmth on the dark roadbed. I slowed for pheasants, flying low from one area of golden grass to another. The males were bronze in the sunlight, their necks ringed in luminous white, the females as buff colored as chaff. Everywhere I looked I saw a sameness of infinite variety.

Not many miles outside the town of Halsey, that sameness ended with a jolt. Trees stood where tallgrass should have been. I had entered the Nebraska National Forest, the largest man-planted forest in the U. S. The woodland stretches across 257,257 acres, including part of the Middle Loup Valley. Crisscrossing the river, which cuts as gray-blue and cold as a flint knife through the golden hills, Highway 2 continued to flank the railroad. I met trains rumbling east, loaded with coal from mines in Wyoming for energy-starved cities on the fringe of the plains.

On down Highway 2, in the heart of western Nebraska where dark blue lakes dot the Sand Hills, a warm wind was moaning through the crumbling ruins of potash factories at Antioch. Few families are left; mostly memories populate the weathered stores and decaying houses. During World War I the town boomed; potash was vital to the manufacture of gunpowder, and Antioch mines operated around the clock to supply train loads of it. The war ended, and people moved on. But the boom had given a proud name to the Sand Hills section of Highway 2—The Potash Highway, so labeled by fence-post signs marked "PH."

A few miles farther west the Sand Hills region tapers off near the point where Alliance begins. The town has been a bustling railroad center since it was settled in 1888. (Continued on page 106)

FOLLOWING PAGES: *Yearlings trail up to a water tank on a range gullied by rain. The wranglers will drive the herd to pasture near Ashby, where each cow grazing on thick summer grass will gain about 275 pounds.*

Converted school bus doubles as a rolling bunkhouse and chuck wagon for hands such as Larry Fleming (right), who herds cattle in the Sand Hills. The routine of hardworking cowboys continues to revolve around trusted mounts and a lean regimen: up before dawn, in the saddle all day, and early to bed. Modern practices, however, increasingly replace old cowpoke ways. Bud Davis (above) shoulders heirloom branding irons that he will heat with a propane torch instead of the traditional wood-fire coals.

"Alliance's claim to fame?" laughed Deb Dopheide, curator of the Knight Museum. "Alliance and Hemingford, a town 18 miles away, argued for years over which one should have the county seat of Box Butte County. Hemingford went ahead and built a courthouse. The towns held many elections, and I'd bet both sides cheated. Alliance won in 1896. I've heard that railroad people who were not even residents of the county voted three or four times."

Outraged, Hemingford sent a delegation hurrying to Lincoln, the state capital, to protest. Alliance quickly made its move. With the help of a railroad superintendent, a group sped to Hemingford by train and stole the courthouse. They raised the building onto flatcars and took off.

"They had to stop several times and widen the railroad cuts," Deb said. "You can still see some of them. But they got it here in one day, on July third, just in time for the big Independence Day celebration. The county treasurer guarded the courthouse with guns and dogs." A grin spread across Deb's face. "They just moved her over and set her down." And there she stayed, a carriage of justice, so to speak, that is argued by townspeople to this day.

On the edge of the Sand Hills where Alliance lies, a different terrain begins. Northward, Highway 2 intersects the Sidney-Deadwood Trail, a wagon route used for shipping gold from the Black Hills after the first strike in 1874. I crossed the Niobrara River, surrounded by rolling

hills and deep canyons thick with evergreens. Dark ponderosa pines soared toward a clear sky. Miles of silence, but for the sound of the wind singing in the pines, led me onto a vast plain punctuated by pale buttes and edged by lofty bluffs. These bluffs mark the beginning of the Pine Ridge, terrain that arcs some 100 miles across northwest Nebraska. They define the northern boundary of the High Plains.

Sioux Indians hunted here until treaties limited their territory and the demise of bison brought increasing hunger. The Red Cloud Agency, a federally funded outpost named for the peacemaking Sioux Chief, Red Cloud, distributed food and supplies to the Indians. Troops stationed at Fort Robinson, established in 1874, protected U.S. interests in the area. The fort spawned nearby Crawford, once a bawdy, bar-filled town, now a peaceful and tree-shaded haven. Newcomers praise clean air and wide vistas, while old-timers prize memories. There, I met a woman whose family history parallels the story of western settlement in Nebraska.

I first saw Lottie Zerbst from behind the etched glass panel of her front door. The glass scene depicted the unfinished U. S. Capitol before 1850, and Lottie's smile shone through where the building's dome would rise. Lottie stands straight, more youthful than her 84 years. She was born in a sod house, slept on a corn-husk mattress, danced to fiddle and mouth harp, and wore flour-sack underwear. "I walked around with the word 'Snow Ball' on my seat for a good many years!" she admitted. "That brand on those sacks just would not wash out."

Her parents had taken a train to Crawford in 1888. Her mother's memoirs describe the trip. The train "was made up altogether of boxcars loaded with all the stock, furniture and machinery that the emigrant wants to bring along to help start on his new venture. The emigrant lived in the way-cars or caboose . . . and had food enough packed in containers to last for the whole trip." Lottie's mother had put their food in the wash boiler. The family's destination was 320 acres of raw prairie.

Lottie shared a poignant story about her father: "In 1875, when he was ten and his brother eight, their new stepmother would have no part of them, so their dad gave them each ten dollars and a sack of sandwiches, told them they were on their own, and sent them on their way.

"They weren't out very many days till Chief Red Cloud and his band picked them up and took care of them. Dad didn't talk much about living with the Indians, only that they were good to him and he learned some Indian language. One of his jobs was sharpening knives for Red Cloud. Dad said the Indians went through many hardships. Years later, they never bothered him because I guess they knew he had grown up among them. If they wanted food, something like that, he gave it to them.

"You didn't dare say anything against an Indian in front of Dad, because if you did you were in trouble. He always felt a part of them. If it hadn't been for the Indians he could have perished easy enough. He knew how it was to be hungry and sleep in a haystack." Her father had worked as a stagecoach driver, a horse-breaker, a roundup cook, and then began ranching. He saw a new wave of people come in to settle free land that the Kinkaid Act opened up in 1904.

Showplace home on Highway 2 in Broken Bow copies a model displayed at the 1904 World's Fair in St. Louis. Early plainsmen built houses with blocks of soil veined with prairie grass. They called the sod "Nebraska marble."

"How my dad hated it when the settlers 'Kinkaided'—began to come in and all these fences began to go up," Lottie said. "People came out from cities. They thought all they needed was a free section of land, and put a cow, a pig, and a chicken on it and they'd make a living for you. Many of the people were not real farmers. They settled where even a jackrabbit would have starved to death. I saw this country settle up, and I saw it unsettle, within a few years. Many folks just couldn't make it."

This land of big sky and dark pines once more attracts settlers. I talked with artists and a businessman, people from the East and West Coasts, who find the sparsely settled Pine Ridge area an idyllic retreat from crowded city life. I left Pine Ridge country with regret, but retraced Highway 2 into the Sand Hills with excitement, for I now followed the eastward-winding trail of another visionary.

On June 14, 1897, Lt. James A. Moss, in command of 20 black enlisted men from B, F, and H Companies of the 25th Regiment, set out from Fort Missoula, Montana, and followed the Burlington railroad line across Nebraska. The detachment was bound for St. Louis, a journey of some 2,000 miles. Each trooper was well drilled, wore a cavalry hat, and carried 39 pounds of pots, pans, blankets, tents, poles, a rifle and 50 rounds of ammunition. The men, however, were not standard cavalrymen.

They rode bicycles.

Lieutenant Moss aimed to prove the efficiency of "the wheel" in military service. His Bicycle Corps endured rain, mud, snow, and heat of 110°F in the shade. On one particular day, when the head wind was light and the road was flat and dry, the cyclists covered 70 miles. On another day, when the road was pure mud, the troopers pushed their bikes only nine miles. The Sand Hills proved their undoing.

"It was impossible to make any headway following the wagon road in loose and often ankle-deep sand," Moss wrote. "The soldiers turned to the railroad right-of-way, bumping over the ties for 107 miles, before they got out of the sand. The constant jar numbed hands and pained shoulders." Intense heat and bad water brought many of the riders to their knees. The bicycle trip took 41 days. Moss's sad summation: "We endured every possible condition of warfare but being shot at."

Parts of that sandy wagon road, which later became State 2 and eventually was paved, still run across the Sand Hills. Like segments of dark blue ribbon draped across crests and flung into valleys, sections of the original road appear on either side or angle beneath the modern highway.

At Ashby, deep in cattle country, I turned north off Highway 2 and followed a paved road. It soon became a gravel road that turned onto a washboard of a sand road; all the roads were former trails across the hills. Collectively, they led me to the Becker ranch. It was November. Indian summer held winter storms at bay. It was time for the autumn cattle drive that would divide the herd for winter pasture.

Pete Becker, three of his daughters, ranch hands, and neighbors had rounded up 811 Black Angus cows and calves and moved them down a meadow to begin a three-day, 35-mile drive to the Beckers' north ranch. Pete's wife, Lassie, and I followed, bumping along in a pickup truck behind an old school bus rigged as a chuck wagon and bunkhouse. I soon fell into the age-old routine of a cattle drive. We always camped near a stock tank or lake, bedded down to coyote songs in the night, and breakfasted by lamplight. I would wake to the sight of young cowboys saddling young horses that bucked in protest, and I would watch cattle slipping through low-lying fog like a dark convoy. We would ride through crisp mornings as hands coaxed, "Yo, cattle; youup, cattle." We would break for rest and a midday dinner, and move through warm afternoons at a steady pace—11 miles or more a day. Sometimes the cattle massed patiently for a gate to be opened; at other times they strung out for two miles down long meadows or across high hills, bawling bovine thoughts.

After the drive I lingered several days in a world of wildlife at the Becker ranch. Coyotes slid glances my way as they slunk between haystacks; mule deer bounded across a hill; muskrats labored at damp lodges in a lake. From the highest hill, Pete, Lassie, and I watched sunset draw russet shadows across miles of golden hills and valleys. Each day grew colder until one morning Pete's words formed crisp clouds as he spoke: "The Canada geese are leaving—means a change in weather."

It was time for me to leave as well. As I reached Broken Bow, snow blanketed the Sand Hills. Near Grand Island, prairie grasses sheathed in ice and frost bent low. I thought of old routes; paths of bison on the move, trails of pioneers with a dream, visionaries' roads to imagined glory. All are segments now of Highway 2. Together they form a trail of vibrant history across Nebraska's heartland.

In the swing of the 1890s, girls at Grand Island's Stuhr Museum wear frontier clothes: calico dresses and a pinafore. The museum honors town growth on the prairie and the settlers who rumbled west by wagon and rail.

July clouds drift above the Buffalo Pasture at Fort Robinson State Park, three miles off Highway 2 on U.S. 20. More than 17 inches of annual rainfall nourish this sprawling grassland, which provides forage for the

park's bison. In central Nebraska (below, right) feathery plumes of foxtail barley, long crusty seed heads of dock, and slender green leaves of sedge make up the habitat of such small mammals as the jumping mouse and the masked shrew.

*Ripe winter wheat bows to a spring
breeze in the Hemingford area.
Nebraska grain fields overlie the
Ogallala Aquifer, one of the most
extensive natural underground
reservoirs in the nation. Many of
the state's farmers employ modern
irrigation devices to tap the deep
supply, while most ranchers prefer
to draw water with the traditional
windmill (right). LeRoy Louden, in
long-sleeved shirt, and ranch hand
Steve Oehler check the oil in the
gear box. "I run more than 1,000
head of cattle," says LeRoy, "and
I need more than 40 windmills
just to keep 'em watered."*

FOLLOWING PAGES: *A solitary box
elder breaks the deceiving spell
of emptiness in the Sand Hills.
Few trees grow naturally in
the Nebraska grasslands. To
supplement nature, state residents
in 1872 founded Arbor Day, a
celebration of tree planting. Today
Highway 2 leads visitors into the
state's central reaches, where the
Nebraska National Forest stands
as the nation's largest
man-made woodland.*

Utah and Arizona Byways:
Touring Canyon Country

By Tom Melham   Photographs by Dewitt Jones

On Scenic Drive in Capitol Reef National Park, visitors pass gaunt ramparts in an area so forbidding that it deterred pioneers until 1871. This corner of Utah stands as the last explored territory in the contiguous United States.

On the map it's just a squiggle that narrows and stops short, a dead end, a thoroughfare to nowhere. And yet this road with no outlet is your passport from the commonplace to the truly awesome.

Lightly trafficked for most of the year, two-lane Arizona Route 67 begins quietly enough in the northern part of the state. From the little town of Jacob Lake it rolls south through tawny seas of grass and thick pine forests that blanket the Kaibab Plateau. Mule deer materialize only to bound off like springbok at your approach, while hawks lazily circle the cloudless blue. But just as the plateau's flowing scenery lulls you into expecting more of the same, the whole world suddenly drops away. Trees and meadows disappear; the gentle Kaibab abruptly plunges off into layered mesas and knife-blade vanes that splinter again and again into ever more numerous and narrow promontories.

Pavement runs out at Cape Royal, a huge overlook on the edge of a spectacular, ten-mile-wide gash in the earth's crust. Here ravens soar in the updrafts hundreds of yards below your feet. A distant roar demands some searching to find the source: green, whitecapped waters of a river glittering through shadows six miles away, *and down*. Welcome to the largest gorge in the world, to a fantasy land of shattered cliffs and crumbling spires, where mundane rock takes on incredible shapes and ever-changing colors. Welcome to the northern rim of the Grand Canyon.

Horizontally, Cape Royal projects into a major bend of the canyon, much as Florida juts into the Atlantic. Vertically, the promontory stands about a thousand feet above the canyon's opposite side. The overlook gazes toward the naturally chiseled stonework on the south wall, as well as the cliff-top village of Grand Canyon and the hundreds of square miles of plateau that sprawl beyond.

Canyon-country byways branch off U.S.89 between Salina, Utah, and Flagstaff, Arizona. News of this region's verdant oases, slickrock castles, and red-rock deserts sped the paving of roads as early motorists clamored for access to such natural wonders as Zion, Bryce, and the Grand Canyon.

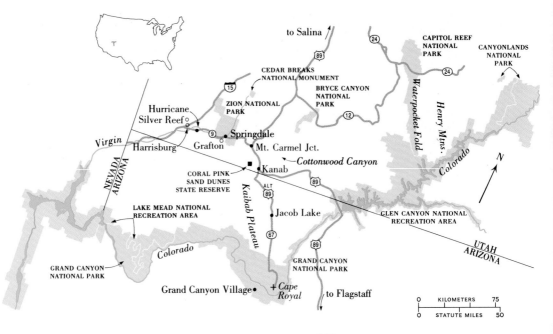

Other North Rim roads roughly parallel Arizona Route 67 and lead to similarly enchanting dead ends. Any one is well worth taking, especially if you arrive as the waning sun ignites both sky and rock; the spectacle transforms crags to glowing coals and casts ever-growing shadows that first highlight, gradually segregate, and inevitably swallow every peak within view. Nightfall at Cape Royal: Only the bright stars and the distant, star-like headlights of cars traveling along the South Rim counter the soft, all-encompassing blackness.

Grand Canyon is the crown jewel of a region often called Color Country. This realm is roughly defined as south-central and southwestern Utah and the Arizona Strip—that portion of the state lying north of the Colorado River. Although politically bound to Arizona, the Strip belongs topographically, geologically, and historically to Utah.

True to its name, Color Country is a rainbow land where dozens of different layers of variously hued rock have been laid down on top of older layers, split by faults, warped into folds, and eroded into spectacular shapes. The region includes some of America's most corrugated and pigmented landscapes. No single road can take you through it all, but then Color Country is so broken and convoluted and unforgettably gorgeous that almost any of its highways qualify as scenic.

For example: While only one highway, Utah Route 9, conveys you to the heart of Zion National Park, half a dozen other roads offer views of Zion's tiered, citadel cliffs that crown the skyline like a rough-hewn and Technicolor version of the Dalai Lama's palace. Utah counts 11 national parks and monuments; no other state contains more federal parks per square mile. Almost half that number stud Color Country: Zion, Bryce, Capitol Reef, Grand Canyon, and others join national forests and state parks in setting aside chunks of this region's gaunt, fetching beauty.

Color Country is a remote land rich in surprise, in slickrock and dense forests, in sandy deserts and churning rivers, in mountains of vivid hue. Such beauty has made it the prime location of many Hollywood westerns filmed for movies and television. This is also the land Zane Grey immortalized in *Riders of the Purple Sage, Wildfire*, and other tales of the Old West. Historically, Color Country has harbored silver mines and Mormon utopias, polygamist cults and outlaw bands, and treasures and traditions real and legendary; some survive even today.

Take the cold October morning when I followed U.S. 89 through Mt. Carmel Junction, Utah, and pulled off into a small draw a few miles south of town. It was a little after 7:30, too early for any highway traffic. Even the sun hadn't gotten up yet; the inky sky had barely begun to lighten along its eastern edge while a westering moon, full and bright, shed a pale and chilly phosphorescence over mesa and plateau. Sunrise wouldn't come for at least another hour, but in that draw six or seven cowboys were making ready without it. They'd already fed their horses and now were trading feedbags for saddles, tightening the cinches as their mounts steamed and stamped. One youth warmed the icy bit of his bridle with a newly acquired cigarette lighter before easing the metal into his horse's mouth. With one foot propped on the bumper of his pickup, Norman Carroll, the boss, chugged the remains of a Coke.

"Just had to wash down that last cup of coffee," he said with a grin. "All we got out here is instant—I can't stand the taste."

Behind him a corral held the reason for being here so early—some 500 head of cattle, a mix of calves, cows, steers, and bulls. Norman and his cowboys had brought them in yesterday from his nearby ranch. Today the wranglers would start their annual cattle drive to Arizona's Kaibab Plateau, where winters are less severe. On the plateau, cattle can graze federal range for less money than it would cost Norman to keep them in hay and to fuss over them with every major snowfall on his Utah ranch.

A casual "I guess it's about time" from Norman got things going. Two cowboys opened the corral gate and began moving out the cattle with shouts and whistles. The cows bawled back, but still got to their feet and slowly headed up-canyon in the predawn gloom. A thin haze of their own freezing breaths hovered above, while curtains of dust began to well up from those two thousand hooves. Packed closely together between steepening walls of the draw, they seemed more a living ooze on the move than individual animals. The riders fanned out behind the herd, their occasional whistles and whoops punctuating the continual background music: a bellowing so intense and mournful you'd swear the cows were being slaughtered on the spot. Norman Carroll's yearly cattle drive had begun.

Many other Utah ranchers also move stock south each fall, but most now truck their beef on the hoof because it's faster and safer. Norman is one of a diminishing breed that clings to the old way.

"It's cheaper," he says, adding that while the 70-odd miles from his ranch to the Arizona range mean a week-long cattle drive, that's no big deal. "We have pretty good feed and water conditions on the way, and . . . well, we just *like* to trail them."

In fact, his cowhands take short wages for their week of frigid nights on the ground and dusty days in the saddle. "They like this getting out," said Norman. "It's a joy." Since so many other ranchers have turned from cowboy power to trucks, he added, the cowboys have fewer chances to use their trail skills. Because part of the cattle drive's route follows side roads that have begun to draw increased auto traffic, Norman eventually may have to truck his herd. He does not look forward to diesels.

"You know, they'll never invent anything that'll take the abuse a cowboy will," he laughed.

Norman should know. Now in his mid-50s, he's been trailing cattle since a boy, when his father, Henry, ran the operation. At age 79, Henry still shows up for the annual drives, although he now rides a pickup rather than a saddle horse. Norman's son, Doug, a banker, is here too. Sure, Norman said, ranching's one way to make a living, but it's also a family thing, generating pride and a life-style, as well as profits.

"It's a good life," he reminisced. "Hard at times, but good."

A different and somewhat headier good life once enveloped the near-by Utah town of Kanab. Until 1984, signs along U.S. 89 at the town's edge billed Kanab as Little Hollywood; for some 40 years, whenever Metro-Goldwyn-Mayer, 20th Century-Fox, and other movie companies wanted to shoot a western in Color Country, they headquartered here.

But don't expect brass stars embedded in the sidewalks; Kanab's heyday is history, although film crews even now occasionally return, and a few mementos of the past persist. The lobby of the Parry Lodge, where actors often stayed, is still walled with their publicity photos. North of town on U.S. 89, the Kanab Movie Ranch offers a touristy collection of rather dilapidated film sets and dramatic natural settings, some not used since the early 1950s. Here you can see, for example, the teetering remains of a narrow wooden bridge connecting two rocky outcrops where the Lone Ranger and Silver triumphed over evil.

Merle "Cowhide" Adams, a lifelong rancher and Kanab resident, recalls the glory days when he hired out to movie crews as guide, stunt man, and double. "I doubled a lot of them guys," Cowhide chuckled, " 'cause they was big and ugly like me. Guys like Bruce Cabot in *Smoky*. And Preston Foster in the 1949 film *The Big Cat*. Of course, back then I had to put a pillow in front to look like Preston. I wouldn't have to now."

At 85 years of age, Cowhide still stands a solid six feet two. He has endured countless fistfights and stampedes, at least one brawl with a 160-pound cougar, and a "fatal" trampling beneath the hooves of a maddened horse—all for the silver screen.

"My 'death scene' took place 'bout 40 years ago in *Smoky*," Cowhide mused. "They paid me $600 for that one bit. And back then a dollar was worth 98 cents."

Cowhide's expertise in riding and roping also won him an off-screen spot coaching child star Roddy McDowall in *My Friend Flicka*. One brief but frustrating scene called for McDowall to lasso the filly's neck. Cowhide recounted:

"Well, I tried and tried to show him, and, hell, the kid would tangle up that rope more than anything. Never could loop it out and throw it anywhere. He was English, you know—you couldn't even understand him." The eventual solution was for Cowhide to stand just off-camera, toss the rope, then quickly hand it to Roddy.

One often used movie setting was Grafton, then and now a Utah ghost town just south of State Highway 9 and west of Zion National Park. Discerning moviegoers should recognize Grafton from such films as *Butch Cassidy and the Sundance Kid*. Remember when the bike-riding Paul Newman, as Butch, freewheels past a schoolhouse that's topped with a cupola, tries to impress Sundance's girl friend (Katharine Ross) with some stunts, and then crashes into a fence? That's Grafton.

Ghost towns are as much a part of Color Country as are its multihued mesas. Places like Silver Reef, Harrisburg, Frisco, Old Irontown, and dozens more offer decaying and abandoned walls as stark testament to a happier past, when the dreams of earlier generations were being realized—or at least actively sought. Many of the towns began as mining camps and lasted only as long as the ore did. Today they draw not only occasional moviemakers and history buffs but also modern treasure hunters, armed with metal detectors and screens to sift through the sandy debris that once was Main Street.

Just east of where Utah Route 9 and Interstate 15 meet lies all that's left of Harrisburg, a farming village that peaked in 1869. Several stone buildings remain. They are remarkably intact despite the perils they've endured, such as fire, falling trees, and time itself. Here I spend several hours with a metal detector, hunting and pecking. Around noon I ponder the morning's take: two handmade nails (old), a brass shotgun-shell casing (new), some broken pottery (probably old), and a 1972 D penny—obviously not dropped by one of Harrisburg's inhabitants, for only ghosts lived here after 1910. My diggings also uncover "desert amethysts," shards of tinted glass, probably from old, colorless bottles turned violet by time. Not much of a haul, and yet I don't tire of the seeking. I imagine that prospectors who panned for gold felt a tingle of anticipation like the one I get every time I set up the machine and start to sweep the ground.

Perhaps I'll have better luck in Silver Reef. The town fronts an unmarked side road northwest of Interstate 15. Still standing here are the red sandstone walls of the building occupied long ago by the banking firm of Wells, Fargo & Company. The company shipped out more than eight million dollars in bullion during the town's first five years. The shipments ended in 1884, when the price of silver dropped to around a dollar an ounce—and even less. Yes, a boomtown gone bust: Silver Reef sits atop what some people claim is the world's only formation of silver-bearing sandstone. It may not yield any ore to me today, but surely I can turn up an old coin or two. The thousand people or so who lived here a century ago must have lost a few. All I'm after is that bit of minted gold or silver that fell unnoticed from a pocket or slipped between the floorboards of a saloon long since rotted away. Out comes the detector.

It can become an addiction, this machine. No matter that the coins continue to elude me even here; every time I unearth another bottle cap or .22-caliber casing and decide to quit, I'm nagged by a conviction that *this* is the place, that I'm just inches from that lost gold piece. Sure, it's easy to laugh at gold fever, but it's easy to catch it too. Who knows? Five minutes more and the detector might even turn up the caches purportedly left by Henry Clark, the town's most famous and successful gambler. He died in a local gunfight without telling anyone where he'd stashed his winnings. Who wants to miss being a millionaire by only five minutes? So I stay a bit longer . . . and find a few more bottle caps.

Of all the Color Country's tales about lost fortunes and buried hoards, none is more fabulous than "Montezuma's Treasure." In the 16th century when conquistadores were terrorizing Mexico, the story goes, some followers of Montezuma realized their leader was doomed; they fled, escaping to the northwest with a huge amount of gold. They crossed the Colorado River with it. When they reached Color Country, they buried their cache, then disappeared.

Around 1918 a more recent chapter in the Montezuma story began to take shape. Whit Robinson, then a boy growing up on his father's ranch ten miles east of Kanab on U.S. 89, remembers:

"I was, oh, 12 years old when this heavy-set, balding stranger showed up at the ranch. Freddie Crystal was his name. He and Bowman —a local store owner—and Dad went off by themselves and talked and pretty quickly came back. Dad informed us that Freddie was going to stay with us for a while. Didn't tell us what his business was, but I think he said he was looking for some kind of manganese ore. I was to be his guide; Bowman was going to grubstake him, and Dad would furnish him a place to stay and a horse. I remember I got five dollars out of it."

Soon, Whit learned that Freddie's interest stemmed not from manganese but Montezuma. He had a photo of what seemed a very old map, devoid of recognizable writing but marked with strange hieroglyphs.

"He claimed he had followed that map out of Mexico," Whit said, "and that someone in Arizona had dug up two or three gold bricks. So he

Waterpocket Fold, named for its natural cisterns, wrinkles the Colorado Plateau in Capitol Reef National Park. Dry streambeds and a few old roads breach the 100-mile escarpment, noted in folklore as an outlaws' lair.

Limestone obelisks reach skyward along "Wall Street" in Utah's Bryce Canyon National Park. Relentless erosion carved this realm of fanciful fissures. A Mormon farmer who staked a claim here in 1875 noted: "It's a hell of a place to lose a cow!" Opposite: Fog drapes the Great White Throne in Utah's Zion National Park.

figured he was on the right trail. The map looked just like the stump of an old tree with dry limbs going off of it."

One day, while searching amid the Vermilion Cliffs northeast of Kanab, Whit and Freddie came upon a bare knoll that gazed across the Cottonwood Canyon area. "It was quite a climb to get there," Whit recalled, "but when Freddie got to looking at that canyon and the white ledges, he figured he didn't need to look anymore." The forlorn topography before them perfectly mimicked the tree-like lines of his map.

Subsequent trips into Cottonwood Canyon took Freddie to a small cave filled with sand. He and a companion dug it out and found a rock wall; they tore it down only to discover a tunnel, also sand-filled, leading farther into the mountain. That night they went into town and hired none other than Cowhide Adams to help excavate. Cowhide remembers:

"That tunnel was practically full of sand. And it had been made with pretty ancient tools, 'cause it wasn't square, just kind of an oval rounding. It was small enough that a man had to have a sawed-off shovel and be on his knees to go into it and shovel that dirt back. There were bones, charcoal, all that sort of stuff in there. And the sand was different from what you'd expect for the area. It had to have been *deliberately* filled in."

Slowly, a shovel at a time, they worked their way into the tunnel. Weeks passed. "Old Fred wouldn't let anybody get in front of him," Cowhide said, "'cause he thought every time he stuck his shovel in that sand there'd be a gold brick on the end of it. We got in there about 20 feet, and all at once a big rock fell out of the right-hand side of that tunnel. It rolled and pinned Fred's leg to the floor. If he'd been alone he'd never got out from under it."

After months of digging, they reached the end of the tunnel. It measured 68 feet long and opened into a large chamber cluttered with more dirt and rubble. Freddie decided he could no longer pay wages, only a percentage. Says Cowhide: "I had my wife Emma and a little boy only about a yearling, and I had to feed them. I needed money, so I left."

Freddie continued, doggedly clearing the room but finding no gold. Discouraged and broke, he left. Since then, five or six other prospectors have taken turns at the site. Some have even filed mineral claims on what maps now call "Montezuma Mine."

To get there, you need a four-wheel-drive vehicle to handle the sandy trail heading up Cottonwood, off the Johnson Canyon road from U.S. 89. You pass bulging, steeply curved cliffs of slickrock, streaked with parallel lines—clear clues that this stone was laid down ages ago by periodically shifting sands. A series of man-made toeholds angles up one rock face; the "Indian stairway," old-timers say, predates Freddie Crystal. You scale the shallow steps, then traverse a slickrock bench to enter a cave several feet wide.

Loose sand forms the floor of the chamber, while the walls are so crumbly you can't tell whether nature or man originally carved them. Indeed, natural caves pock this same sandstone formation elsewhere in the canyon; dozens of holes mark this very cliff, *(Continued on page 133)*

Architect of Zion, the snowy Virgin River hides behind cottonwood, box elder, and ash. Swollen in spring, the stream (opposite) flows past a landmark trio: the Great White Throne (left), the Organ (center), and Angels Landing.

Emmy-winner Bob Davison takes a break with a badger that he nursed to health after it had been mauled by a predator outside Zion. The animal shares starring roles with Bob's puma (below, left) in the filmmaker's wildlife productions.

FOLLOWING PAGES: *Bleak rim of Point Supreme in Utah's Cedar Breaks National Monument borders a three-mile-wide natural amphitheater of limestone. Oxidized iron and manganese stain the distant tiers.*

some no larger than a basketball, some man-size and leading farther into the rock. Ahead, even without a flashlight, you can see the beginnings of all sorts of side passageways leading off the main one. Your thoughts turn to Freddie and the excitement he must have felt here before he realized that no fortune awaited him in the sand-filled darkness. The others who followed him found numerous Indian relics, but not a nugget of treasure. Still, tales of Montezuma die hard here. Whit and Cowhide agree that if gold ever was cached in this canyon, it still remains.

"No one's found it yet, but someone will," Cowhide insists. "There's *something* there."

One possibility is uranium, which became a local rage during the atomic-energy consciousness of the 1950s. As always, Cowhide rode with the action, hiring out as a guide for a prospecting company.

"We flew all over," Cowhide said, "everywhere within a hundred miles or so of Kanab. They had a little Piper Cub with a nucleometer and scintillator all on the back seat. Every time we went over Cottonwood Canyon, it'd knock the needle right off both of them outfits. You'd get down on the ground, and you couldn't find a damn thing."

Possibly Cottonwood Canyon harbors two bonanzas—one of gold, one of uranium. But don't bet on it, for when it comes to treasure, the only kind you can count on out here is the scenic sort. Color Country is loaded with it, and you don't need a shovel; everything's right on the surface.

"There's so much here," says Jane Whalen. She's with the Southwest Resource Council, an environmental group headquartered in Hurricane, on Utah Route 9 near Zion National Park. "A lot of visitors just go to a few of the better-known national parks and think they've seen it all. Don't get me wrong—the parks are great. But there's so much more."

Enough so that a lifetime seems too brief to explore it all. There are, for example, the Henry Mountains—the last range mapped in the contiguous 48 states. Home to bison and cougar, these granite slopes stand out in a realm of mostly sedimentary rock. There are canyons: Robbers Roost, Paria, Escalante, and many others crease Color Country; some are so narrow that you can touch both sides at once. There are cliffs: the Blue Hills and the Hurricane Cliffs, in addition to the Vermilion, White, and Pink Cliffs. Each represents the exposed edge of a different, uptilted geological stratum that underlies plateaus north of the Colorado River.

And don't bypass the Waterpocket Fold, a prolonged rocky spine ridging nearly a hundred miles of the Colorado Plateau north of Glen Canyon, in south-central Utah. Named by explorers who found pools of water trapped amid its convolutions, this stone rainbow displays 15 or so different formations worked into delicate hues and varied shapes.

Most of the Waterpocket lies within a showcase of Utah slickrock often missed by sightseers: Capitol Reef National Park. Both the fold and the park run long and narrow, roughly north to south. Utah Route 24 cuts across this axis, providing the park's main entry; the road traces an uptilted and rapidly changing land of surreal scapes, carved and painted by nature's own Dali. Colors are vivid or subtle, arranged in thin laminates or broad swaths. Gravelly mesas, totally bleak and ravined by time, rise

---

Stocky bristlecone pine grows best in the worst soil and weather conditions found in the rocky, arid, windswept area of Cedar Breaks. These trees gain only an inch in girth each century, but some have lived nearly 5,000 years.

like miniature mountain ranges: You could just as well be looking down at the Rockies from 30,000 feet.

As you proceed southwest, roadside cliffs grow more interconnected and castle-like, creating the feel of a fortified and forbidden city. A row of small and angular promontories guards one rock wall like so many stone lions before a library. Hoodoos and rock goblins haunt a stretch of corduroyed badlands robed in orangy reds and tans. Shaly purples and greens merge with deep red sandstones that grade into pale pinks and paler lavenders. There are also blind arches: Gothic spires and vertically ridged walls that mimic the ornate facades of Victorian architecture.

What did those pioneering Mormons, who fled west in the 1840s to escape religious persecution, first think of this alien land? It was so unlike their Midwest homeland. This new realm bore no green plains or hardwood forests; it was arid and stark, studded with one strange, upswept sculpture after another. And yet for the Mormons it became Zion.

Today, long after Brigham Young led them into Utah's valley of the Great Salt Lake, Color Country continues to astound. True roads, such as Arizona Route 67, now maze much of this former wilderness. But nature has left the land so broken that no highway system can reach every niche, and many unspoiled areas remain accessible only by horse, helicopter, or hiking boot. To really sample this land, you must explore as those first settlers did, daring beyond the beaten path, trusting to foot and fate. After all, every ending is also a beginning, and here in Color Country many a dead-end road leads you to some of the most dramatic and hauntingly wild terrain anywhere in the United States.

The Sunday calm of Hurricane, Utah, settles on Main Street. During the work week, business in town picks up as tourists arrive on State 9. The two-lane road follows the North Fork of the Virgin River through Springdale (opposite) toward the banded cliffs of Zion National Park.

Buckaroo Doug Cox, 9, carries a makeshift crop during a drive along a storied route, the cattle trail. The 500 bellowing Herefords will take a week to move from a ranch in Utah to milder winter pastures on the Kaibab Plateau in Arizona. Below, Doug and wrangler Rolland Hoyt savor a less dusty tradition of the cowboy's vanishing life-style—swapping tall tales.

Grand Canyon's North Rim view scans two billion years of geologic time. The mile-deep rift of layered rocks includes pale limestone mesas and reddish sandstone terraces. Opposite: Long ears gave mule deer their name.

FOLLOWING PAGES: *Desert shrubs, mule-ears collar sand eroded from cliffs edging Utah's Coral Pink Sand Dunes State Reserve, 12 miles off U.S.89.*

U.S. 89:
From Glacier to Yellowstone

By Jennifer C. Urquhart   *Photographs by Dewitt Jones*

Legacies of the Ice Age: Sharp ridges, scoured valleys, and such angular mountains as Flinsch Peak in the foreground create the majestic wilderness that U.S.89 travelers find in Montana's Glacier National Park.

"I think the land has shaped us, this combination of mountains and plains," said A. B. Guthrie, Jr., shifting in his chair slightly. I was west of Choteau, Montana, at the home of the prize-winning novelist. Bright and witty at 82 years of age, Bud Guthrie was telling me about the land where he had grown up. "I like to get close to the mountains, but I like to have eye room too. I don't like to be shouldered by mountains."

To the west the craggy peaks of the Rocky Mountain Front checked my line of sight, but to the east I had eye room aplenty; my glance could travel across undulating prairie clear to the horizon. It was August, and I was following U.S. 89 across Montana, meandering between Guthrie's mountains and plains.

U.S. 89 is not a modern road. Its precursor in Montana was the Y-G Bee Line, a dirt road—oiled and graveled in places—completed in the 1920s as a highway connecting Yellowstone and Glacier. Today the 380-mile section of the road between the two national parks is paved, and for the most part two lane. From Choteau, I drove north toward Glacier. Few roads serviced the park until 1933, when the 51-mile Going-to-the-Sun Road opened the heart of Glacier's wilderness. The highway was a tremendous engineering feat in its day. Most of the work had to be done during the short summer seasons. Supplies often had to be carried up the steep terrain by pack mule. Men used muscles and crowbars to move huge boulders and blasted with dynamite to cut a roadbed in the cliffs.

I turned off U.S. 89 onto the Sun Road and entered Glacier from the east. I stopped briefly at an overlook and admired the view. Ice-sculpted peaks, jammed one upon another, rose beyond a wide valley. I drove on and crossed the Continental Divide at Logan Pass, the center of the park. A couple of miles beyond I came upon hundreds of streams braiding their way down a slope called the Weeping Wall. Wildflowers speckled every patch of green. Here on the western slopes of the Divide the parkland seemed less stark, its hills more rounded under thick forest.

For a closer look at this country I planned to follow a well-known trail from Logan Pass. During my visit with A. B. Guthrie, I had accused him of inventing the Big Sky, the title of one of his most famous novels and a popular label for Montana. "I didn't invent it." He smiled. "It was there!" But this particular afternoon at Logan the open sky was hiding, and Going-to-the-Sun seemed a misnomer. Clouds dipped menacingly over rocky cliffs. The wind picked up, and at this elevation of a mile and a quarter, the air felt cold, perhaps in the low 50s. Rain began pelting me.

I layered myself in sweaters and jackets and walked to the head of the Highline Trail. In the days before the Sun Road, hiking or horseback riding were the only ways to reach this remote area. Visitors would stay at chalets and tent camps along the trails. Even today most of the park is accessible only by paths. My plan was to hike seven and a half miles on the Highline to Granite Park, one of two chalets still operating.

Chalet personnel had assured me that there would be plenty of hikers on the trail and that I would find company. I wondered what kind of company they meant as I neared an orange sign that displayed a drawing

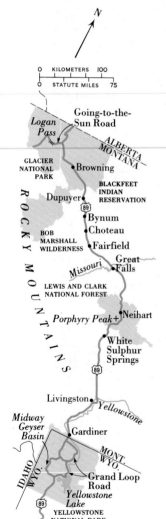

Vacation highway, U.S. 89 annually moves a million motorists to Glacier and Yellowstone National Parks in Montana and Wyoming. Sections of the road parallel ancient Blackfeet trails and historic rail lines that carried gold and silver miners northwestward through forests, ranges, and farmlands.

of a fierce grizzly. "Be Alert," it warned. A second sign elaborated: "Do not travel alone. Make your presence known by noise." There was not a soul in sight. Perhaps I'd find people ahead. Almost immediately a cloud of fog swallowed me. Being alert wouldn't do much good.

Noise, the sign had said. I played a Chopin tape in a little recorder I was carrying. Its volume was too frail against the blustery wind. I resorted to clapping my hands and nervously singing "Marching to Pretoria." If anything, my out-of-tune voice should scare the bears away . . . I hoped.

I must have walked a mile down the trail when I heard voices. I hurriedly caught up with a family from British Columbia, Margaret and Larry Moore and their twin teenage girls. The wind had cleared the last wisps of fog, and a rainbow of wildflowers appeared along the trail. I forgot about the bears as Margaret pointed out Indian paintbrush, asters, columbines, and oxeye daisies.

As we climbed higher, we entered a world of mountain sheep and goats. A ram peered down from a boulder five feet away. Ewes browsed among the rocks, paying us no heed. "They're used to hikers," a passing park ranger explained. Farther along the trail in a lush meadow, two nanny goats calmly turned their long, white-bearded faces toward us. Their kids gamboled by their sides, kicking and butting.

The Moores had to turn back to Logan, and I was alone again. A couple in their 70s appeared around a bend and came toward me. "Did you scare the bears away ahead?" they asked, half in jest, as they passed. Our uneasiness was not entirely fanciful. Glacier has a lot of grizzlies, and they are unpredictable. Steep mountain topography tends to throw bears and people onto the same paths.

It was getting late, and the daylight was fading. I hurried on through heavy brush, anxiously singing my marching song as loud as I could. At last a steep-pitched roof peeked above the crest of a ridge. Soon I was eating homemade soup, soothing nourishment for my song-weary throat. I was in the main room of Granite Park Chalet with 40 other guests. Some 2,000 pounds of food and supplies are hauled in by horses each week. College students and other young people handle the daily chores, which include baking all the bread and pastries in a propane-fueled kitchen, laundering linens in a wringer machine, and lighting the candle that provides the only illumination in each of the dozen bunk rooms.

After dinner we sat outside watching the sunset. Conversation turned to the grizzly. "Man has an atavistic fear of the grizzly from prehistoric days," said Bob Litchfield, a ranger who keeps his eye on the bears for the park. A high school teacher from California, Bob was spending his sixth summer at Glacier. "It's not so far from teaching to bear management. It's really people management," he said. "The bears have been managing themselves forever."

The main goal, I found out, was to keep people and grizzlies apart and to make sure that the bears did not learn to depend on the garbage and food in the camps. As darkness fell, the evening chill drove us inside shivering to bunks piled high with blankets. The next morning I scrambled up a talus slope behind Ron Jong and Tom Morris, two geologists on a hiking weekend. Ron had worked in this region for three and a half years. We picked our way across slippery stretches where water seeped from glaciers and snowfields. "This area is part of the Siyeh Formation. Precambrian—it's more than a billion years old," Ron said, touching a coarse rock. "In this rock you can find stromatolites, which are probably

Glacier's varied life forms each possess survival tricks supplied by nature. Although August still holds an alpine meadow at Lake Ellen Wilson (opposite), a mountain goat browses in a new woolly coat that will counter winter's chill. Plump from summer feasting, a Columbian ground squirrel (below, left) stores the fat that it lives on during eight cold-weather months of hibernation. Dense sprays of Lewis monkey flowers and other highland vegetation (below) have mastered fast living. In Glacier's brief growing season many plants have only sixty frost-free days to complete their life cycle.

the flare of our campfire. We watched the rising moon fade the brilliance of the Big Dipper and Cassiopeia.

The next day we took a switchback trail up Crazy Creek, traversing a near-vertical talus slope. At first I could look back calmly into the gaping valley. Then the trail, looking ever smaller hundreds of feet below us, became unnerving. "I never believed I'd end up doing something like this," said Hal, a surgeon in everyday life. At last we reached a flat ridge, skirted a patch of perpetual snow, and lurched down a steep slope into a basin called the Valley of the Moon. After dinner we lingered around the campfire, quietly chatting and savoring our last night on the trail.

U.S. 89 loses touch with the mountains near Great Falls, Montana's industrial heart. But just south of the "Electric City," so dubbed because of power generated from a series of falls on the Missouri River, the road twists and squeezes through the Little Belt Mountains. This range yields a different kind of gold than do the grain fields to the north. Decades ago, rich mineral strikes here helped earn Montana its nickname, the Treasure State. I drove through a pine-forested canyon to Neihart, once a hub of mining activity. "Within our hill lies wealth untold," a local poet sang in 1896, "Of Silver bright and Yellow Gold." In those days Neihart stretched a mile along the road and numbered around 3,000 people. Today fewer than 100 remain. But, with vacation homes and renewed interest in a few

of the mines, a revival of sorts is under way. Just outside Neihart, miner Ray Vipperman took me into the old Florence mine. "Right now we are pumping water out of the mine so we can sample the ore to be sure it's still worth mining," Ray said. "The Florence claim was staked in 1886. It was mined on and off for 50 years. It only went to 500 feet, but the workings yielded silver worth hundreds of thousands of dollars."

Some people find a different treasure in mountains along U.S. 89. "If only I could just go off to a mountaintop somewhere," Joy Rose used to wish when her children were small. Now, the Connecticut housewife was doing just that, as a volunteer fire lookout for the Lewis and Clark National Forest. To meet Joy, I climbed the tower atop 8,192-foot Porphyry Peak, near Neihart. "My daughter calls this my tree house," Joy said. "When it's clear, I can see 130 miles, all the way to Canada." She had reported no fires this summer, but in 1984, the following year, she would report one. The blaze was part of a fiery rampage ignited by lightning and fanned by the wind. The conflagration destroyed *(Continued on page 156)*

Wheat stubble and fallow land stripe fields in north-central Montana. An annual harvest totaling about a hundred million bushels of wheat and barley enriches this seven-county grain region known as the Golden Triangle.

Hutterite women turn their backs on individuality. They always dine separately from men in this commune along Montana's U.S.89. Each child (opposite) in the colony, however, begins learning Christianity in a coed kindergarten.

FOLLOWING PAGES: *A gentle ridge shelters a farmstead from stiff prairie winds in north-central Montana. A homestead act in 1909 expanded settlement in the area. Immigrants—Irish, Germans, Norwegians—came to farm the rich glacial soil.*

a quarter million acres of woodland, prairie, and ranchland throughout much of Montana. "The lightning, it's scary!" Joy told me. Her 55-foot tower has four lightning rods, but to ensure her safety during an electrical storm Joy has to sit in the middle of the room on a wooden chair with its legs set in four chunky, old-fashioned glass insulators.

I climbed down from Joy's aerie, drove out of the Little Belts onto the open plain, and turned in at a gate just north of White Sulphur Springs. Howard Zehntner met me at his house. Beyond stood the old farmhouse where he'd grown up. "It's log under the tar-paper siding," he said. "It was so cold in winter. You could throw a cat through the wall just about any place." Howard and his two brothers raise cattle on lands their Swiss grandfather homesteaded in 1878. Sections of old U.S. 89 cut through the

---

Velvet coat of skin and fine hairs covers the antlers of a Yellowstone bull moose. The velvet peels off at the start of rutting season in fall. Antlers bared, males begin to spar one on one, a prelude to combat in winning a mate.

farm; Herefords grazed where the middle of the old road had been. "I remember when it was a gravel road," Howard said. "Each time they straightened it, they kept eating more of our meadow. But now they have cut a good route that misses our place."

Beyond White Sulphur Springs, I passed through Ringling, Wilsall, and Clyde Park—communities Howard calls "poke-'n'-plumb towns": Poke your head out of the window, and you're plumb out of town. To the east I could see a dusting of early snow on the Crazy Mountains. Ahead in the distance lay Paradise Valley. Gold-tinged clouds and mist veiled the Absaroka Range; the sun broke through, and a rainbow, then two, arched before me. U.S. 89 merges with Interstate 90 for a little while here and snakes upstream along the clear green waters of the Yellowstone River into Livingston.

Born of a railroad in 1882, Livingston is still tied to one. On tracks along Park Street, trains of the Burlington Northern come into town for repairs. Maintenance shops for the rolling stock remain the major employer in the region. In a huge overhaul shop, grease-smudged men worked on behemoth locomotives. The din was deafening, the acrid smell of hot metal searing. Whistles and bells shrilled as an overhead crane swung a 21-ton diesel engine, like a plaything, the length of the building.

Along Livingston's side streets a quiet contrast flourishes. Writers, artists, filmmakers, and actors frequent cultural corners. Galleries and boutiques prosper between old bars and sports and fishing stores.

As for recreation in Paradise Valley, my favorite stop was Chico Hot Springs, south of Livingston, on the east side of the Yellowstone. In the 1860s, gold miners scrubbed their clothes and bathed in these hot springs. Today the soothing waters massage the aches and pains of tourists. The hot springs give only an inkling of the geothermal power concentrated farther south in Yellowstone National Park.

Just outside Gardiner, near the border of Montana and Wyoming, U.S. 89 runs under a stone arch, the grand entrance into Yellowstone. A "howling wilderness of three-thousand square miles, full of all imaginable freaks of a fiery nature" was Rudyard Kipling's impression of Yellowstone in 1889. Once inside, U.S. 89 loses its identity to other park roads, including the Grand Loop—a drive that curls for 142 miles across an astonishing landscape. I parked in the Mammoth Hot Springs area and climbed wooden stairs to Minerva Terrace. Rome's Trevi Fountain can't compete with these baroque forms of calcium carbonate, shapes that constantly change as water from subterranean limestone beds wells up and deposits minerals on the surface, forming huge terraced pools.

Poking along past lakes and through groves of lodgepole pines, I paused at geysers and mud pots and hot springs of every color. Fumaroles blasted away like devilish furnaces. At Midway Geyser Basin, I studied a vast field of steam plumes and was overwhelmed by the thought that here, not many miles below the earth's surface, there churned a furnace of molten rock, or magma. Groundwater seeping near the magma superheats. Some of the water flashes into steam. Pressure changes. Suddenly a geyser erupts, spewing hot vapor, water, and a sulphurous smell into the air. More than 200 active geysers vent Yellowstone's fury. Kipling was right: ". . . miracles pall when they arrive at the rate of 20 a day."

My journey across Montana had been on nearly empty roads. My trip through Yellowstone was a different story. Sightseeing motorists jammed the roadway. But in such a large wilderness area it is not hard to get away from the crowded roads. In Lamar Valley, in the northeastern part of the park, I mounted a horse, rode across a sprawling meadow, and met Sam Moore to spend a quiet day fishing on Slough Creek. Few fishing areas

FOLLOWING PAGES: *Progression of lodgepole pines in Yellowstone continues as seedlings sprout where old logs lie. The trees acquired their name because Indians used the slender young trees for the framework of their lodges.*

offer anything comparable to the clear air and mountain-fed lakes and streams in this corner of Wyoming and Montana. Sam, a Texan from El Paso, prepared a Green Humpy—a fly made of elk hair and green thread. He spotted a fish. With an expert flick of the wrist he whipped his fishing leader and line in broad S-curves over his head and cast. The fly kissed the water with the lightness of a feather, then vanished in a thrash of water. Sam's reel buzzed, and he pulled in a beautiful native cutthroat trout, about 18 inches long. Obeying the stream's "catch-and-release" regulation, as well as the highest code in the sport of angling, he gently put the fish back into the water and tried for another.

Many activities besides fishing await Yellowstone visitors who are willing to venture off well-worn trails. "Most people don't get far from the road," says Rick Reese, director of the Yellowstone Institute. "Here at the institute we offer courses that range from wildflowers to grizzly bears, from canoeing to bicycling. We get people out doing things."

On a frosty September morning I joined seven others in a course called "Biking Yellowstone." We would cycle 45 miles that day. We pedaled past Yellowstone Lake, then crossed the broad Hayden Valley, where bison and elk grazed. The name "Yellowstone" probably finds its origins in the golden bluffs that line portions of the river. But in early fall the whole park takes on a tawny glow.

Bicycling is not really new here. Bikes, in fact, preceded automobiles in the park by many years. Not until 1915 were cars legally admitted. Our cycling course ran beside the Yellowstone River from Yellowstone Lake to Artist Point, near the center of the park. As we pedaled along, the roar of rushing water grew louder. We were approaching the Upper Falls of the Grand Canyon of the Yellowstone River. Not far beyond this spectacular drop the river would take a mightier plunge in one of Yellowstone's most beautiful settings. The Lower Falls would plummet farther than Niagara. We hurried to Artist Point to see the panorama of the canyon framing the Lower Falls, a now-famous scene captured on canvas in the 1870s by the painter Thomas Moran. On the high rim the river seemed to hesitate, then its jade-green water turned a frothy white as it cascaded in a feathery plume 308 feet to the canyon floor.

Two six-year-old boys next to me discussed the golden hue of the canyon walls, streaked pastel by iron oxides. "You know what you should call that mountain there?" one asked, then answered himself—"Candy Rock Mountain!" A man from Idaho leaned against the guardrail and said, "You can't get too much of this place." He was right.

As U.S. 89 led me away from Yellowstone, the end of my journey, I began to understand more fully what A. B. Guthrie had been talking about. The open, kindhearted people out here have been shaped by their land, an expansive region of mountains that don't hem them in and plains that give them plenty of eye room.

During the snow season, park animals such as the bison find warmth and exposed vegetation in Midway Geyser Basin and other Yellowstone hot spots.

FOLLOWING PAGES: *Hayden Valley slumbers under winter's blanket, while a pine awaits the company of July wildflowers in its Yellowstone meadow.*

Scalding water constantly gushes from the earth at Mammoth Hot Springs. Each day the upwelling deposits two tons of minerals that create crusty terraces (opposite). Heat-tolerant algae paint the ever-changing contours. Yellowstone fumes with more than 200 active geysers. Despite geologic disruptions, some caused by regional earthquakes, Old Faithful (below) has varied its average interval of eruptions less than 15 minutes in the last 100 years. The famous fountain performs about 20 times a day, spewing thousands of gallons of hot spray more than ten stories into the air.

FOLLOWING PAGES: *"The setting sun shining into the spray and steam ... gave it the appearance of burnished gold...." Great Fountain Geyser, which inspired these words in 1869, still dazzles travelers in the wilds of Yellowstone.*

California 1 and U.S. 101:
Traveling the Sunset Coast

By Toni Eugene   Photographs by Dewitt Jones

Storm clouds roll toward Cypress Point on the Monterey Peninsula. Along California's Pacific shore, Routes 101 and 1 provide sweeping views of a coastline weathered by the eternal assault of wind, rain, and wave.

At times the lane ahead had lost the battle with waves and weather and crumbled at the water's edge. In other places the entire road retreated inland. Nevertheless, starting at Oregon's southern border, I drove almost 800 miles on U.S. 101 and California State Route 1. Dazzling sunsets and crashing waves blazed my course for six weeks as I curved beside the Pacific on my way to Santa Barbara.

From giant redwoods to palm trees, the two roads pass rocky headlands, sandy beaches, urban sprawls, and wilderness strands unspoiled since Spanish explorers first viewed them more than 400 years ago. Pavement where pavement is not meant to be, I sometimes thought. Yet surely no other highways unite mountains, sea, and shore as do 101 and 1.

I began my trip on a rainy day in late September, and minutes south of the Oregon border, near Crescent City, I had to slow for a crew replacing the right lane of U.S. 101. A high tide had taken part of the road with it. Fifty yards west, the Pacific foamed over fangs of stone. Harbors rife with rocks, violent seas, heavy fogs, and merciless storms make the northern California coast perilous. In 1865 a gale shoved the steamer *Brother Jonathan* onto a reef north of Crescent City. That wreck, the greatest maritime disaster in the state's history, drowned 213 people. In 1964, seismic sea waves triggered by an Alaskan earthquake killed 11 people and destroyed half the town; undaunted, Crescent City rebuilt.

Twenty miles to the south, the same year the earthquake hit, the Klamath River overflowed and wiped out its namesake town. The afternoon that I drove into the area the river, as well as the ocean, was peaceful. Along this strip of narrow beaches U.S. 101 is a winding and hilly two-lane road, with an extra lane for passing. It gets plenty of use as cars play tag with 18-wheel trucks hauling redwood logs. The road grew out of a series of wagon trails and became known as the Redwood Highway in the 1920s for the trees that crowd it. Flowing through the timber are fast streams that offer some of the best salmon fishing in the United States.

Lee Weaver, a logger who has lived in Klamath all his life, took me to one of his favorite fishing holes on the river. Upstream we killed the motor of Lee's boat and floated quietly. On the nearby bank, redwoods, fir, and spruce glistened in the late afternoon sun. As we baited our hooks with cured salmon roe, Lee nodded toward a deep pool near a jumble of rocks. "That should be good," he said. "Salmon like these holes." We cast, and I payed out line slowly. "If you feel a tug," Lee said, "pull the line in sharply to set the hook, but don't jerk it or you may lose the fish."

Within minutes the line went taut, then arced with tension. "Reel in," Lee coaxed. "Keep the line taut, but don't pull too fast." I reeled in slack, and the fish came closer. Too fast. The reel whirred as the salmon turned and ran with my line. He was farther away than ever, and I started over. Carefully I reeled in just enough to keep the line taut, and just enough to bow the rod. The fish came closer, then streaked off again. Suddenly he arched out of the water—a streak of silver against dark green.

My wrist started to ache, and I propped the pole on my hip. "Hang on, he's getting tired," Lee said. *He's* getting tired, I thought. This battle

---

Seaside highways: U.S. 101 winds south from the grasslands of the Oregon border. At Leggett, California State Route 1 picks up the seacoast to Gaviota Pass. The roads cover 788 miles along a varied landscape of farms and forests, beaches and palisades, cities and bays, headlands and harbors.

had been going on for half an hour. I raised my rod high, reeling in to bring the salmon's head out of the water as I pulled it close. Lee reached down, scooped it into a net, and brought it, flopping wildly, into the boat. We cleaned my catch back at the boat ramp.

"How big is he?" I asked.

"Oh . . . about 14 pounds," Lee said, "and 26 inches long."

On the Klamath, where sunset in the redwoods is a prize in itself, even a novice can catch a fish that experienced anglers would envy.

At seven the next morning, fishermen were already out when I crossed the Klamath. Mist wrapped the hillside redwoods in gray gauze and muted the engines of logging trucks struggling up the crooked grades of U.S. 101. Redwoods—resistant to fire, rot, and insects—are valuable timber trees. Nature limits them to a section of coast 500 miles long and about 30 miles wide. Frequent summer fog, moderate temperatures year-round, and ample winter rainfall foster their growth. A century of logging has destroyed 85 percent of the old-growth stands, but many of the trees are now protected. Redwood National Park, the largest preserve, incorporates three state parks and covers 106,000 acres.

With Jean Swearingen, a National Park Service employee, I entered the park to see the world's tallest tree. From an access road eight miles east of U.S. 101 we hiked more than a mile down a steep trail. Shafts of sunlight pierced the cathedral hush of the forest. The fresh tang of redwood needles mingled with the strong scent of damp earth. Rust-colored sparrows chattered at our intrusion, and at a bend in the trail two black-tailed deer bolted away into the depths of the sanctuary.

The path flattened out at a grove where redwoods soar so high that it is almost impossible to comprehend their height. Jean walked up to the base of the tallest giant and touched its soft, reddish-brown bark. "This tree is more than 600 years old. Its trunk is about 44 feet around," she said. The redwood measured 367.8 feet tall when it was discovered by NATIONAL GEOGRAPHIC naturalist Paul A. Zahl in 1963.

Outside the park, we passed areas where loggers had removed all the trees. These clear-cuts were brown wastelands littered with stumps and branches. Redwood sprouts growing as high as six feet in one year from the stumps will cover the scars. But it could take 500 years for the new redwoods to reach the heights of their felled predecessors. Few trees have piqued tourist curiosity more than those south of Eureka, where U.S. 101 parallels the 33-mile-long Avenue of the Giants. Along this route billboards advertise a tree you can drive through, a one-log house, and such redwood souvenirs as bowls, plates, and carved statues of Indians.

At Leggett, U.S. 101 turns inland, and another road—Highway 1—picks up the coast. The route tops rugged oceanside cliffs at Mendocino, a logging town founded mainly by New Englanders in the 1800s. Here gray stone walls red with geraniums fence clapboard galleries, antique shops, and artists' studios painted soft greens, blues, and browns. I watched the colors mellow in the dying light as the sun melted into the ocean, briefly staining the water scarlet. Few other highways in the nation run where the day closes with such a fiery light.

Before dawn the next morning I met Steve Sinclair, a guide with Force 10 Ocean White Water Tours, in the nearby community of Elk. "The way to see the Mendocino coast," he assured me, "is from the water." Shortly before sunup, I struggled into a wetsuit and safety vest, and at daybreak we maneuvered Steve's two-man kayak into the water. Both air and sea were cold. We bobbed through breakers, then cleared piles of gray rock. Steve did most of the paddling; I was lost in the scenery. Above us Highway 1 was a narrow thread hanging on the very rim of land—so close I could see the logging trucks barreling by. In a cliff ahead of us a black hole in the gray rock grew larger as we approached.

"The ocean has cut lots of caves in this area," Steve said. "I call this one Cuffey's Cut. The water is low enough now that we can go in safely." I ducked as we plowed into the cave. Pale green water and dark rock entombed us. In the damp blackness, swells rocked the kayak. "At high tide it's dangerous to come in here. The ceiling's too low." Steve's voice boomed off the water-worn walls.

We slipped out of the cave into bright sunshine and paddled close to a truck-size boulder covered with scores of California sea lions. Some, draped like limp sausages, slept. Others barked, plunged into the water, then clambered back to their perches to repeat the performance.

Surging waves squeezed into a hole in the rocks to our right and forced a roaring geyser 30 feet high. A bank of fog rolled in from the open ocean, and a 15-foot breaker raced toward us. "Paddle hard for shore," Steve ordered. I did—fast. But before we could turn, the wall of water hit us, and we climbed straight up. Suddenly I was paddling air. We had bounced high out of the ocean. I froze, one hand clutching the paddle, the other the gunwale. I was certain we were going to capsize. *Smack!* We landed flat on the next wave. The impact knocked my breath away. I gulped for a few seconds and forced myself to loosen my grip on the kayak. I looked over my shoulder at Steve. "Wake you up?" he asked.

The lunging surf and rocky shoreline along the northern coast have endangered seamen since 1542, when Portuguese navigator Juan Cabrillo sailed from Mexico and became the first European to discover California. For more than a century, lighthouses have helped sailors navigate these waters. Off Highway 1 south of Elk, at Point Arena, a 115-foot white tower houses a powerful seacoast beacon. The original lighthouse, built in 1870, was destroyed by the San Francisco earthquake in 1906 and replaced by the present structure the following year.

Coast Guard Boatswain's Mate Jerry Bell was looking after the light station. "It can get pretty rough out here," he told me. "Last January we had winds up to 112 miles an hour." I followed him up the 117 steps to the top of the tower. "The day of the old-fashioned lightkeeper is almost over," Jerry said. "There're only 37 or so manually operated lights left in the U.S. All of California's lighthouses operate automatically now."

South of Point Arena, Highway 1 rolls across hills toward Tomales Bay. Opposite the narrow inlet is a hooked sliver of California called Point Reyes. This hammer-shaped peninsula breaks into the Pacific for ten miles and features Point Reyes National Seashore, a windswept park of meadows, wilderness beaches, and dense forests that cover 71,000 acres. On the point's northwest coast, where steep arroyos and bluffs collapse into the sea, the collision of the cold California current with the

---

Twin cascades of Nojoqui Falls in Santa Barbara County race gossamer rivulets that filter down 180 feet through a carpet of moss and fern.

FOLLOWING PAGES: *Coastal fog nourishes rhododendrons and redwoods. Many of the trees—the world's tallest—exceed heights of 300 feet.*

warm, moist coastal air makes many Point Reyes mornings foggy. The clouds usually burn off by noon, only to return by evening. Early one morning, on my way to the Morgan horse ranch near park headquarters, I found that the misty realm of solitude and subdued sounds has a delicate beauty and appeal. Out of the fog came soft chirping, calls from some of the 400 species of birds on the peninsula. Little brush rabbits hopped through the beam of my headlights.

The fog had lifted by the time I reached the ranch, where National Park Service equestrians train Morgan horses and teach rangers to ride. Prized for their versatility and endurance, Morgans are the only U.S. breed of horse whose ancestry can be traced to a single sire, the famous Justin Morgan of Vermont.

Ranch manager Gina Muzinich and I rode our Morgans up a trail edged with huckleberry bushes and California bay trees. We dismounted atop 1,407-foot Mount Wittenberg, the peninsula's highest point. The peaceful grassy valley that anchors the view from the summit understates the fact that the depression is Point Reyes's visible expression of the San Andreas Fault. This great crack in the earth's surface slipped as much as 16 feet here during the San Francisco earthquake, one of the worst temblors in U.S. history. The dark line of Highway 1 dips across the deceptive valley floor and links white dots of distant houses. Beyond, brown hills reach eastward like the fingers of a spread hand.

The ranchland of Point Reyes adjoins the inviting beaches, windy headlands, and urban parkland of the Golden Gate National Recreation Area (GGNRA). Founded in 1972, the GGNRA encompasses 72,815 acres of state parks, surplus military land, Alcatraz Island, and the Golden Gate Bridge. Beyond Stinson Beach, part of the 28 miles of shoreline in the GGNRA, Highway 1 edges steep cliffs. At an overlook I parked to admire a hawk gliding on updrafts and watch red sunlight play on breaking waves. Beyond the water San Francisco—small pale boxes backed by white skyscrapers—marched up and down rolling hills.

I pulled back onto the highway. The six lanes of the Golden Gate arched ahead, suspended by cables from two orange towers 746 feet tall. For decades people had dreamed of spanning the mile-wide entrance to San Francisco harbor, but tides, winds, and rocks daunted engineers until 1933, when work started on the great structure. Although construction proved difficult and dangerous, costing the lives of 11 workers, the bridge was completed in four years.

As traffic swept me across the Golden Gate, I glimpsed Alcatraz on my left. A ferry ride, the only way to reach the island, takes about eight minutes. I made the crossing and wandered through the crumbling cell blocks of dank steel cages that once held the most notorious public enemies in the United States. Alcatraz, which began its history as a fort in 1854, served as a federal penitentiary from 1934 until 1963. Al Capone, George "Machine Gun" Kelly, and Robert "the Birdman" Stroud were among 1,573 criminals who served time on the Rock. Its catwalks and gun towers are empty now, but the island, one of San Francisco's most popular sites, attracts half a million tourists each year.

Beyond the Golden Gate, Highway 1 cuts through western San Francisco. Bright flowers in the urban playground of Golden Gate Park made me decide to stop in the city for a picnic. The park was sand dunes a century ago, but imaginative plantings of trees, gardens, and lawns transformed it into a three-mile green swath from the heart of the city to the

Pacific. In the park's Japanese tea garden, orange carp flashed in a pond shaded by blue irises. Ducks floated on a lake fringed with red and white impatiens. Throughout the park, people were strolling, biking, roller skating, sailing Frisbees, and playing touch football.

Below San Francisco, Highway 1 slows through suburbs until housing developments give way to ranches and plowed fields. About 50 miles farther south, sandpipers playing tag with the surf brought the spell of the ocean back to me. Mostly freeway in this area, Highway 1 bends with the shore of Monterey Bay and traverses coastal plains planted with strawberries and feathery-leafed artichokes.

The town of Monterey, once the capital of California, was the principal port in the state before gold was discovered a hundred miles west of San Francisco in 1848. Tourists, writers, and painters discovered the seascape of Monterey early; Robert Louis Stevenson lived here in 1879. Sardine fishing and canning were the major industry in the mid-1930s, when 19 canneries lined the bay for a mile. Immortalized by John Steinbeck in his novels *Tortilla Flat* (1935) and *Cannery Row* (1945), Monterey today is a mixture of beautiful old adobe houses, modern hotels, souvenir shops, restored restaurants, and warehouses facing the wide curve of the bay. But when Steinbeck and a friend, artist and writer Bruce Ariss, arrived in the '30s, the town was very different.

"Monterey," Steinbeck wrote, "sits on the slope of a hill, with a blue bay below it and with a forest of tall dark pine trees at its back." The hill "where the forest and the town intermingle, where the streets are innocent of asphalt and the corners free of street lights" was Huckleberry Hill, which became part of Steinbeck's Tortilla Flat.

"When my wife and I built our studio up there in the pines we had no gas or lights," Bruce told me. "Cannery Row down there on the bay was a mess—loud, smelly, and dirty. By 1950 the sardines had disappeared, and the canneries closed. But Steinbeck made Monterey famous. The revitalization of the row as a tourist center began about 1960."

Seventeen Mile Drive on the Monterey Peninsula has been famous much longer. Tourists used to ride along the bay in carriages to admire the groves of Monterey cypress and the sea lions and pelicans on Seal and Bird Rocks. Now the drive is a toll road within Del Monte Forest. This resort contains elegant homes and condominiums and five 18-hole golf courses, which include the prestigious Pebble Beach Golf Links.

Not far south of Seventeen Mile Drive I stopped at Point Lobos State Reserve. Ranger Jerry Loomis showed me a grove of Monterey cypress so dense their windblown crowns blocked the sun. Lacy pale green lichen dripped from twisted branches and dark needles. The restricted habitat of redwoods seems boundless compared with that of the cypress. These trees, native only to Monterey County, cling to less than 50 acres. Their tortured trunks and gnarled limbs testify to the battle they wage with wind and storms to survive on the area's last ledge of land.

"Point Lobos has been a state park since 1933," Jerry said. "When 750 submerged acres were added to our onshore acreage in 1960, Lobos became the first underwater reserve in the nation."

The park allows limited diving at two coves, Whalers and Bluefish. Jerry handed me a guidebook he had put together. Captioned color photographs sealed in plastic pointed out the park's *(Continued on page 183)*

Isolated at high tide, Battery Point Lighthouse off Crescent City becomes accessible at the ebb. Visitors reach the station, which doubles as a museum, by walking out 200 yards across a tombolo, or sandbar from the mainland. Below, far right: In Bodega,

St. Teresa's has served worshipers for more than a century. Spanish rule planted Christianity in California in 1769, and Franciscan friars nurtured it by building a coastal chain of 21 missions.

Natural and man-made beauty: Sweeping cables of the Golden Gate Bridge gracefully carry six lanes of traffic and two sidewalks over the strait that links the Pacific with San Francisco Bay. Not far north of this span built of steel lies a long strand constructed by nature, Point Reyes National Seashore (opposite). The peninsula attracts city dwellers with forests of Douglas fir, bluffs, dunes, and abundant wildlife such as northern harriers, tule elk, and gray whales that swim within sight of the wide beach. At the shoreline with Kathy Stevens and its young master, Brian Kavanaugh-Jones, Iza joins in the fun of barrel-walking.

181

natural sunken treasures. I put a copy of the book in a net bag, adjusted my scuba gear in the frigid waters of Bluefish Cove, and followed Jerry's fins downward through a forest of waving brown kelp. We dove to a depth of 80 feet. Ocean swells rocked me as I thumbed through the guidebook and identified the marine life on a gray stone outcrop: orange feather duster worms, flat red bat stars, purple coralline algae, and the waving pink tentacles of strawberry sea anemones.

From Point Lobos, Highway 1 enters Big Sur country, where broad headlands and irregular coves are relentlessly being carved by the onslaught of sea against land. In this area, convict crews took 9 years to chisel nearly 90 miles of Highway 1 from the abrupt descent of the Santa Lucia Mountains to the Pacific. The laborers completed the job in 1937. The route is the only road through these tortuous miles, which give you the feeling that you are driving at the end of the earth. Jagged mountains thrust from the sea. Granite cliffs, grassy hillsides, and rocky beaches border the road, and in many spots, bluffs on the right shoulder plummet hundreds of feet to the water. In places, the road's two lanes dip within 50 feet of pounding surf; elsewhere they zoom almost 1,000 feet above sea level. Cars become dwarfs in this world of giant scale.

The route straightens through the narrow Big Sur Valley, population center of this isolated fragment of coast. Along the Big Sur River, motels and restaurants hug the road. Elsewhere few houses intrude, clinging on the brink of cliffs or nestling in hollows. Only about a thousand people inhabit this coast, and they all cherish their solitude.

William Brainard Post, a Connecticut sailor, homesteaded here in the 1860s. His great-grandson, Bill, who lives near the original redwood-frame house, can remember seeing construction crews blast Highway 1 through Post land. "Before they built the road," he said, "a drive to Monterey—about 35 miles—took several hours."

The clash of ocean and land responsible for Big Sur's wild beauty wreaks havoc with transportation along this eroded shoreline. Each year winter rains cause mudslides that close sections of Highway 1. About 35 miles south of Carmel, I braked in front of a massive landslide that had been squatting on the highway for the past seven months. The displaced dirt from a towering bluff spread across the road for about 600 feet and formed a hill about as high as the Empire State Building. Gary Saunders, a regional manager for the California Department of Transportation, stood with me at the foot of the bulky roadblock and shook his head. "I've been with the department 22 years," he said, "mostly with this cow trail. We always have problems—40 road closures in 1982—but this is the worst I've seen. About three miles of highway is missing."

The coast becomes even more secluded in the area of Jade Cove. I stopped here on a high bluff and picked my way down to a black sand beach cobbled with rocks. Below the turquoise waves in the cove lies nephrite, a mineral in the jade family suitable for making ornaments. Ken Comello earns part of his living from the rocks.

Sycamores share a field of winter wheat with a couple in Santa Ynez Valley.
In addition to ample crops of grain and grapes, this mountain-sheltered
basin raises such prized horses as Thoroughbreds and Arabians.

"I find my best jade by scuba diving," he told me. "There's lots of it underwater. But the cove is rough. Winter and spring storms kick up heavy surf, and kelp growth is heavy in summer." Some of the nephrite boulders on the floor of the cove measure more than ten feet long and weigh hundreds of pounds. To raise them, Ken attaches nylon bags to the rocks, then inflates the bags with air so that the lumps float to the surface. With the help of some friends, he carries the rocks up the cliffs.

In a small workshop behind the gas station and restaurant that are the community of Gorda, Ken works with huge hand-built saws. Slowly he

slices the boulders into thin slabs, which he polishes and crafts into gleaming coffee tables. He tumbles and smooths smaller bits to make belt buckles, necklaces, rings, and key chains. On my way south of Gorda I passed many shops that sold such jewelry, some of it Ken's work.

Below Gorda, twin ivory-colored towers rising within sight of the highway announce San Simeon, the lavish estate of millionaire publisher William Randolph Hearst. He called his house "the ranch." Others, impressed by its opulence and its hilltop eminence, called the 115-room structure "the castle." Seven years after Hearst's death in 1951, his residence became a state historical monument.

The 123 groomed acres around the castle display botanical wonders ranging from fan palms, spreading oaks, and Italian cypress to smaller plantings, including hedgerows of trimmed boxwood and wide beds of roses. Norman Rotanzi, supervisor of the grounds, has tended the plantings at San Simeon for almost 50 years.

"When Mr. Hearst lived here, there were about 25 gardeners," Mr. Rotanzi said as we strolled through the beautiful rose gardens. The yellow, red, pink, and white blossoms were still wet from an early morning shower. "We planted four to five thousand trees every year for a decade. Mr. Hearst was the chief landscape architect. We'd be working, and he would come over a ridge and join us, wearing a $200 suit full of burrs." Mr. Rotanzi pointed to a cerise blossom. "That Charlotte Armstrong is 35 years old . . . old for a hybrid tea rose. I remember when we planted it. The gardens were planned so something was always in bloom. Mr. Hearst liked to keep the flowers in their natural setting. Guests had to go outside to see blossoms; we never had bouquets in the buildings."

Inside, the castle tells more about Hearst. Mixed with silver, tapestries, and priceless works of art, overstuffed furniture covered in chintz reveals his penchant for informal comfort amid stately splendor.

Rolling ranchland reaches from Highway 1 to the ocean south of San Simeon. The road turns inland at Morro Bay and temporarily merges with U.S. 101 at San Luis Obispo. Green signs identify this leg of the route as part of El Camino Real—the Royal Road—because it closely follows the original road that linked Spanish outposts in California. In 1769 Spanish priests began a chain of 21 missions along the coast. San Luis Obispo developed around one of the churches in 1772. Still the center of town, Mission Plaza encloses a manicured park hemmed with modern shops and dominated by the mission's beige adobe walls and red-tile roof. Those curved tiles, which replaced the original grass roof destroyed by flaming arrows during an Indian attack in 1776, became a popular part of mission-style architecture that spread throughout the Southwest.

Geographically, northern California becomes southern California at a rocky cape just west of Gaviota Pass, where Highway 1 and U.S. 101 come together again. Here the coast swings sharply eastward and angles away from the Pacific's battering. Rough seas, fogs, and winds pushing down from the north are diminished by the rugged headland, and the battle between land and sea eases to a friendly rivalry.

A superhighway out of Gaviota, U.S. 101 speeds between the Santa Ynez Mountains and the sandy shore for 30 miles to the stucco walls and red-tile roofs of Santa Barbara. This is southern California's northernmost city. With its soft sunshine, waving palm trees, and casual air of affluence, Santa Barbara stands in striking contrast to the rockbound northern coast of thick fogs, timber towns, and fishing villages.

The beginning of southern California marked the end of my journey. I pulled off the road, parked at a beach, and for a while watched the cars traveling north. I envied those travelers their adventures and discoveries on U.S. 101 and Highway 1, routes that writhe across the very edge of land to bind sea and shore, city and country, old and new.

Adobe arch near Lompoc frames visitors at La Purísima Concepción, largest of California's Spanish missions. The churches used clay tiles to replace thatch roofs, targets vulnerable to Indians attacking with flaming arrows.

FOLLOWING PAGES: *Artichokes blanket a field south of Carmel. California fills most of the U.S. demand for this plant's edible cluster of floral buds.*

Bird Rock teems with gulls and cormorants—as well as sea lions. After breeding in
the warmer waters of Mexico and southern California, many of these marine mammals
take up residence on Bird Rock off the Monterey Peninsula, where rich feeding grounds
offer hake, salmon, and anchovy. With coin-operated binoculars from a parking lot on

Seventeen Mile Drive, tourists can watch the sea lions sunning on the 50-foot-high outcrop. Lolling on the beach at Año Nuevo State Reserve in San Mateo County, a two-month-old elephant seal lifts a flipper to catch the cool sea breeze.

Oldest and only
seaside amusement park
remaining in California,
the Santa Cruz Beach
Boardwalk flags a crowd
with the sign of its most
popular attraction:
the Giant Dipper.
The 60-year-old ride,
aficionados say, ranks as
one of the world's ten best
roller coasters. Another
thriller, the Jet Star
(opposite) turns knuckles
white with fast dips and
steep curves. High-fidelity
entertainment at the beach
blares from a "box"
(below) toted by a
barefoot music lover.

Fine-textured dunes of Pismo State Beach surround early morning riders. Joe Hartnell (far right) manages livery stables that rent to visitors who want to explore the sandy expanse on horseback. Some sightseers prefer dune buggies. This area remains one of the few places in California to allow vehicles on the beach.

FOLLOWING PAGES: *At last light, California's captivating beaches—such as Arroyo Burro at Santa Barbara—tempt travelers to stop and look to the sea for its essence. It's calm or violent, never boring, and, like the passage of life along Routes 101 and 1, ever changing.*

Notes on Contributors

LESLIE ALLEN graduated from Bryn Mawr and worked as a free-lance writer before joining the Society's staff in 1978. She has covered Tierra del Fuego, maritime preservation, and the Chesapeake Bay for the Special Publications *Secret Corners of the World*, *Preserving America's Past*, and *America's Hidden Corners*.

Photographer TERRY EILER combines a teaching career in visual communications at Ohio University with free-lance assignments. For the Society, he has focused primarily on "closed society" peoples, including Eskimos, Hopis, Navajos, and the Havasupai.

A graduate of Gettysburg College, TONI EUGENE joined the Society's staff in 1971. She has written picture captions for many Special Publications and is the author of the children's book *Strange Animals of Australia*. Her byline appears in the Special Publications *America's Wild and Scenic Rivers* and *Exploring America's Valleys*.

RALPH GRAY completes 42 years of service with the Society in 1985. Editor of the children's magazine *WORLD* since its inception ten years ago, he formerly edited its predecessor *School Bulletin*. In 1962 he covered U.S. 89 from Mexico to Canada for NATIONAL GEO-GRAPHIC. His road assignments for the magazine also include the Lincoln National Memorial Highway and U.S. 40 from the Atlantic to the Pacific Coast.

California-based photographer DEWITT JONES holds a master's degree in filmmaking from UCLA. He concentrates on North American landscapes, and has been a regular contributor to the Society's publications for 13 years.

CHRISTINE ECKSTROM LEE majored in English at Mount Holyoke College. Since joining the Society's staff in 1974, she has coauthored the Special Publication *America's Atlantic Isles* and has written chapters for the Special Publications *Mysteries of the Ancient World*, *Isles of the Caribbean*, and *Exploring America's Valleys*.

For 14 years staff writer TOM MELHAM has covered topics as diverse as coral reefs and the history of America's cars and airplanes. His contributions include chapters in the Special Publication *Alaska's Magnificent Parklands* and the large-format book *The Desert Realm*. He wrote the Special Publication *John Muir's Wild America*.

CYNTHIA RUSS RAMSAY, a native New Yorker on the staff of Special Publications since 1966, has traveled extensively and has written about geology, mountaineering, history, and archaeology. Her byline appears in many Special Publications, including *America's Spectacular Northwest* and *Alaska's Magnificent Parklands*.

Staff writer GENE S. STUART, who studied art history and archaeology at the University of Georgia, worked several years on the Yucatán Peninsula in Mexico. She wrote the Special Publication *The Mighty Aztecs* and coauthored *The Mysterious Maya*. Her children's books include *Secrets from the Past* and *Three Little Indians*.

JENNIFER C. URQUHART is a graduate of Smith College, where she majored in history and English. She began her career with Special Publications as a researcher in 1973. She wrote the children's book *Animals That Travel*, and has contributed to TRAVELER magazine and to the Special Publication *America's Wild and Scenic Rivers*.

On the Special Publications staff since 1977, SUZANNE VENINO has written a number of children's books for the Society, including *Amazing Animal Groups* and *What Happens in the Autumn*. She explored prairies and badlands during her chapter assignment for the Special Publication *America's Hidden Corners*.

STEVE WALL, a free-lance photographer living in Virginia, has covered the Chattooga River and Vietnamese refugees on the Gulf coast of Mississippi for NATIONAL GEOGRAPHIC. His first work for Special Publications appears in *America's Wild and Scenic Rivers*.

Zion-Mount Carmel Highway in Utah curves toward peaks leached white by seeping water. Rivers and rainfall through the ages carved these mountains from the Colorado Plateau.

NATIONAL GEOGRAPHIC PHOTOGRAPHER GEORGE F. MOBLEY

Composition for Exploring America's Scenic Highways *by* National Geographic's Photographic Services, Carl M. Shrader, Director, Lawrence F. Ludwig, Assistant Director. Printed and bound by Holladay-Tyler Printing Corp., Rockville, Md. Film preparation by Catharine Cooke Studio, Inc., New York, N.Y. Color separations by the Lanman Progressive Company, Washington, D.C.; Lincoln Graphics, Inc., Cherry Hill, N.J.; and NEC, Inc., Nashville, Tenn.

Library of Congress CIP Data
Main entry under title:
Exploring America's scenic highways.
   Bibliography: p.
   Includes index.
   1. United States—Description and travel—1981- .
2. Roads—United States—Guide-books. 3. Automobiles—Road-guides—United States. I. National Geographic Society (U.S.). Special Publications Division.
E169.04.E86 1985   917.3'04927   84-27268
ISBN 0-87044-479-4 (regular edition)
ISBN 0-87044-484-0 (library edition)

Index

Boldface indicates illustrations.
Italic indicates illustration captions.

Acknowledgments

The Special Publications Division thanks the individuals, groups, and organizations named and quoted in the text for their assistance during the preparation of this book. The poem quoted on page 57 is "Breaths," by Birago Diop, with music by Ysaye M. Barnwell: © Barnwell's Notes Co. 1980. The editors also acknowledge the expert help of personnel of the American Automobile Association, Blue Ridge Parkway Association, Galena Historical Museum, National Arboretum, National Park Service, Nebraska Department of Economic Development, Smithsonian Institution, U.S. Army Corps of Engineers, and the following individuals:

Chapter 1: Stephen C. Harper, Dr. Harold A. Meeks, Candy Moot, Donald H. Remick, Russell C. Smith. **Chapter 2:** John Davis, Gary Everhardt, Mary Jaeger-Gale, Hugh Morton, Freeman Owle, Dr. Daniel Pittillo, Harris Prevost, Dr. Cratis Williams. **Chapter 3:** Dr. Jeffrey P. Brain, Ray Claycomb, Dr. Patricia Galloway, Dale Smith, Jim and Debby Tully. **Chapter 4:** Michael Douglass, Michael Doyle, John Edman, Robert Fisher, Fred Funk, Donald Jonjack, Henry Schneider, Robert Smith. **Chapter 5:** Veldon and Wanda Morgan, Levi Richardson, Curtis M. Twedt, Tom and Twyla Witt. **Chapter 6:** Clay Alderson, George Davidson, Dr. Wayne K. Hinton, Victor Jackson. **Chapter 7:** Joan Anzelmo, Richard B. Berg, Clyde Lockwood, Cliff Montagne, Norma J. Tirrell, Amy Vanderbilt, Dave Walter, Dan Wenk. **Chapter 8:** Alan Baldridge, Tomi Kay Lussier, Sudy Macdonald, Joan Duren Pease, Norman Root, Stephen Veirs, Wayne Wheeler.

Additional Reading

The reader may wish to consult the *National Geographic Index* for pertinent articles, and to refer to the following:

Chapter 1: Charles W. Johnson, *The Nature of Vermont*; Gale Lawrence, *Vermont Life's Guide to Fall Foliage;* Christina Tree and Peter Jennison, *Vermont: An Explorer's Guide.* **Chapter 2:** Jerome Dolittle, *The Southern Appalachians*; Harley E. Jolley, *The Blue Ridge Parkway*; Duane H. King, *Cherokee Heritage*; William G. Lord, *Blue Ridge Parkway Guide.* **Chapter 3:** Jonathan Daniels, *The Devil's Backbone*; Robert V. Remini, *Andrew Jackson and the Course of American Empire, 1767-1821*; Douglas Waitley, *Roads of Destiny.* **Chapter 4:** Jane Curry, *The River's in My Blood;* Stephen Feldman and Van Gordon Sauter, *Fabled Land/Timeless River;* Timothy Severin, *Explorers of The Mississippi;* Mark Twain, *Life on the Mississippi.* **Chapter 5:** Bruce H. Nicoll, *Nebraska, A Pictorial History;* James C. Olson, *History of Nebraska;* John David Unruh, Jr., *The Plains Across;* D. Ray Wilson, *Nebraska Historical Tour Guide.* **Chapter 6:** Charles S. Peterson, *Utah, A History;* Ward J. Roylance, *Utah: A Guide to the State;* Angus M. Woodbury, *A History of Southern Utah and Its National Parks.* **Chapter 7:** Asa Brooks, *Following Napi: Glacier National Park through the Eyes of a Ranger-Naturalist;* Douglas H. Chadwick, *A Beast the Color of Winter;* Hugh Crandall, *Yellowstone: The Story Behind the Scenery;* Clark C. Spence, *Montana: A Bicentennial History;* Ann and Myron Sutton, *Yellowstone: A Century of the Wilderness Idea.* **Chapter 8:** Madge M. Caughman and Joanne S. Ginsberg (editors), *California Coastal Access Guide;* Augusta Fink, *Monterey County, The Dramatic Story of Its Past;* Tomi Kay Lussier, *Big Sur, A Complete History and Guide.*